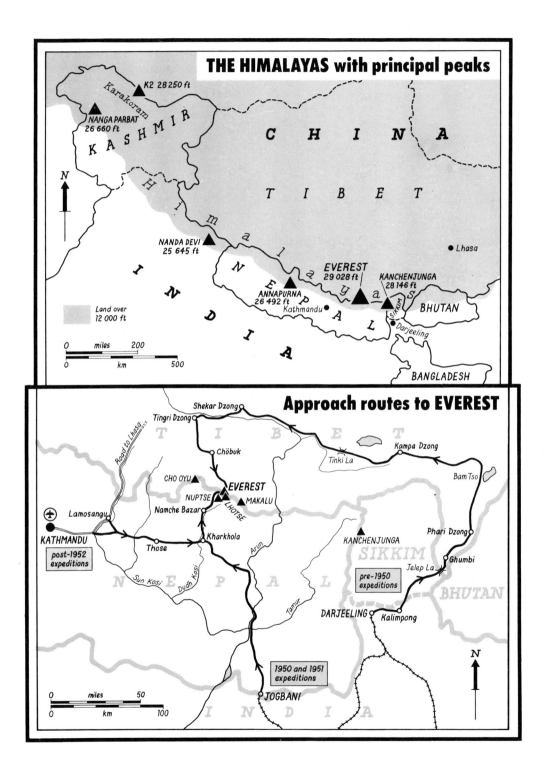

THE HIMALAYAS with principal peaks

K2 28 250 ft
Karakoram
NANGA PARBAT
26 660 ft
KASHMIR
CHINA
TIBET
Himalaya
N
NANDA DEVI
25 645 ft
NEPAL
EVEREST
29 028 ft
KANCHENJUNGA
28 146 ft
Lhasa
ANNAPURNA
26 492 ft
Kathmandu
SIKKIM
BHUTAN
INDIA
Darjeeling
Land over
12 000 ft
miles 200
km 500
BANGLADESH

Approach routes to EVEREST

Shekar Dzong
Tingri Dzong
TIBET
Road to Lhasa
Chöbuk
Kampa Dzong
Tinki La
Bam Tso
CHO OYU
EVEREST
NUPTSE
MAKALU
LHOTSE
Lamosangu
Namche Bazar
KATHMANDU
Kharkhola
Phari Dzong
post-1952
expeditions
Those
Arun
KANCHENJUNGA
SIKKIM
Ghumbi
Sun Kosi
Dudh Kosi
NEPAL
Jelep La
BHUTAN
pre-1950
expeditions
Tamur
DARJEELING
Kalimpong
1950 and 1951
expeditions
N
miles 50
km 100
JOGBANI
INDIA

10ᵒᵒ

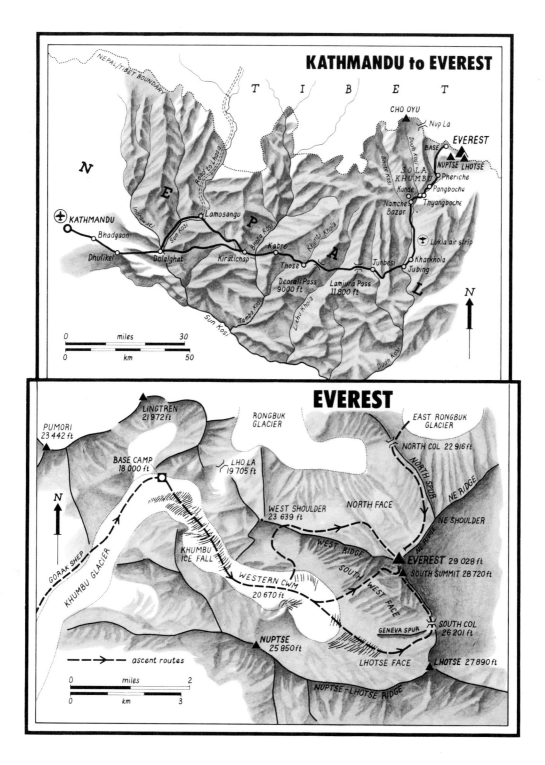

KATHMANDU to EVEREST

T I B E T

NEPAL/TIBET BOUNDARY

CHO OYU
Nup La

EVEREST
BASE
NUPTSE LHOTSE

Road to Lhasa

Dudh Kosi

Bhote Kosi

SOLA
KHUMBU

Pheriche

N

Kunde
Pangbocha

E
Namche
Bazar
Thyangboche

KATHMANDU

Bhadgaon
Indrawati

P
Lamosangu

Lukla air strip

Dhulikel
Dolalghat
Sun Kosi

Sun Kosi

Bhote Kosi

Kabre

Kiratichap

A
Kharkhola

Junbesi
Jubing

Those
L

Deorali Pass
9000 ft

Lamjura Pass
11800 ft

Likhu Khola

Khimti Khola

Sun Kosi

Tamba Kosi

Likhu Khola

Dudh Kosi

N

miles   30
0

0   km   50

EVEREST

LINGTREN
21972 ft

RONGBUK
GLACIER

EAST RONGBUK
GLACIER

PUMORI
23 442 ft

BASE CAMP
18 000 ft

LHO LA
19 705 ft

NORTH COL 22 916 ft

NORTH SPUR

NE RIDGE

WEST SHOULDER
23 639 ft

NORTH FACE

N

WEST RIDGE

NE SHOULDER

GORAK SHEP

KHUMBU
ICE FALL

NE RIDGE

EVEREST 29 028 ft

SOUTH SUMMIT 28 720 ft

KHUMBU GLACIER

WESTERN CWM
20 670 ft

SOUTH WEST FACE

GENEVA SPUR

SOUTH COL
26 201 ft

ascent routes

NUPTSE
25 850 ft

LHOTSE FACE

LHOTSE 27 890 ft

NUPTSE-LHOTSE RIDGE

miles   2
0

0   km   3

EVEREST

Goddess of the Wind

EVEREST

Goddess of the Wind

RONALD FAUX

Chambers
EDINBURGH

Cover: Everest
(*Photograph John Cleare*)

Facing title page: The South West Face
and west flank of Everest, rising behind
an icy spur of Nuptse.

After title page: Natural sculpture in the Ice Fall.

After contents page: Climber in the Ice Fall.

Facing introduction: The first view
of Everest (with its plume) from above the
Dudh Kosi river — about 35 miles of sight.

© Ronald Faux 1978

First published by W & R Chambers Ltd 1978

Made and printed in Great Britain by
T & A Constable Ltd, Edinburgh

ISBN 0 550 20361 3 (cased)

Contents

Introduction

The moment that a distant black triangle of rock straddling the border of Nepal and Tibet was pinpointed as the highest summit on earth, Mount Everest was established as a clear goal for adventurers. The *Goddess of the Wind* had little hope of being left in peace. Even so, for thirty years after the first serious expedition the mountain resisted all attempts to reach the summit and by that time Everest had generated its legends, heroes and literature.

Even today when jet travel, colour television and the passage of many pairs of boots to its summit have robbed Everest of its remoteness and mystery, the mountain continues to beckon climbers and to fascinate those who would not for the life of them set foot on steep ground.

The early, heavily grained photographs retain a magical quality, showing indistinct figures toiling towards the North Col in tweeds and World War I gaiters; climbing Everest in the same nailed boots used to walk up Snowdon.

Some of the pioneers shunned the use of oxygen equipment — indeed it was so cumbersome and inefficient in those early days that to be without it was arguably an advantage. They reached altitudes which are still phenomenal and those first attempts are remembered with admiration for the men whose names are now cut into the history of the mountain: Mallory, Odell, Norton, Somervell, Irvine and their many companions. They went to Everest when it was totally unknown and the dangers of climbing at high altitude were not properly appreciated.

Since those times climbers of many nationalities have attempted the mountain; almost seventy people have reached the summit by an increasing variety of routes and there is a long waiting list of people who wish to try.

The climbing techniques which have made it possible to conquer hard routes on lower mountains are now used on Everest and the achievement of the British South West Face Expedition in 1975 was an important breakthrough in mountaineering development.

The achievement on Everest which has brought history on the mountain nearly full circle and which may pacify the purists who object to the use of gadgets is, as Mallory put it, a 'gasless' ascent without the use of oxygen equipment. Reinhold Messner, the eminent mountaineer from South Tyrol who has specialised in climbing without aid to high altitudes, believed this to be the ultimate mountaineering goal. On the twenty-fifth anniversary of the first ascent of Everest, he and Peter Habeler, an Austrian, successfully made such an ascent, supported by an Austrian expedition on the South Col Route.

Everest still offers some open challenges. The first traverse from the North East to the South Col Ridges will depend on political permissions rather than technical difficulty. An ascent of the South Col route (the supposedly easy way up the mountain) by a small expedition, without the massive support which every previous attempt has had, has yet to be made. The New Zealand bid in 1977 was a brave move in this direction. Finally, the Kangshung Face from Tibet would be a tremendous, though risky undertaking.

But by whatever route and whichever means, Everest will clearly remain a destination for generations of mountaineers yet to come.

EVEREST

The ultimate mountain, or merely the highest?

Nowhere else is more ferociously hostile. Everest is the polar cap without air, and tilted so that a slow, orderless cataract of ice-blocks grinds, cracks and mutilates its way down into the stale tongue of the glacier below. The cataract is called the Ice Fall and there is a graphic simplicity about the name; ton upon million ton of young ice thickly layered in the Western Cwm is pressured to the edge of the 2000-foot drop where it fractures into massive slabs, pristine white on top and shading to the colours of chilled steel where the raw depths are exposed. Day and night the movement is as implacable as a nuclear reaction. The ground shudders, grumbles edgily to itself and suddenly opens up a new chasm or closes an old one. Tall towers of ice topple with an explosive roar, huge embankments collapse in self-consuming fury, filling the air with flying particles of ice and the climber with a solemn awareness of his mortality. When climbing the mountain from the south, the Ice Fall is an unavoidable part of Everest.

Base Camp, the point where the Cook's tour ends and the serious business begins, is a ragged sprawl of bright tents clustered on a shamble of rocks at the foot of the Ice Fall. The rocks border the glacier which creeps imperceptibly past. It is an impressively beautiful place if one can ignore the piles of rubbish from several decades of mountaineering expeditions.

At sunset the cold nips ears, nose and any exposed skin. From the communal tent comes the smell of the evening meal being cooked, and a warm flood of light from the hurricane lanterns. Ducking under the canvas entrance and the signs which warn off the stream of trekkers who arrive unwanted, the blast of warmth is welcoming. Skin made taut and sensitive by keen wind and sunglare stings with the change of temperature. Hot soup feels as if it is cauterising cracked lips. Conversation is terse, people are wrapped up in their own thoughts. Loads are handed out and orders given. The morning call will be at 5 o'clock.

From the luxurious down folds of a sleeping bag the morning summons is rudely intrusive. 'Cha, sahib,' the voice says and a teapot penetrates the tent flap, steaming cheerfully. It is a painful, cruel awakening in the grey

Climbers set out on the hazardous route through the Ice Fall. Towering above them, the West Shoulder of Everest.

Base Camp, 'a ragged sprawl of bright tents clustered on a shamble of rocks at the foot of the Ice Fall'.

light; the difference in temperature inside and outside the sleeping bag is grotesque. Long-johns are pulled over goose-pimpled limbs. Our legs are thinner now, more wiry, and the convivial fullness around the waistline has been erased. The doctor has warned us that from this point we begin to deteriorate and we shall not start to recover until the thick, richly oxygenated, lowland air spreads through our bodies again.

This will be my first climb through the Ice Fall. What will it be like? I tell myself: 'Pull on the double-lined boots, wriggle your toes in the cold, stiff leather and search with the torch for the rest of the kit; crampons, over-boots, duvet jacket, mittens — don't forget them — axe, snow goggles — high priority — and that daft-looking hat covered in pastel-coloured flowers that you bought from the Nepalese Hat Shop in Kathmandu.'

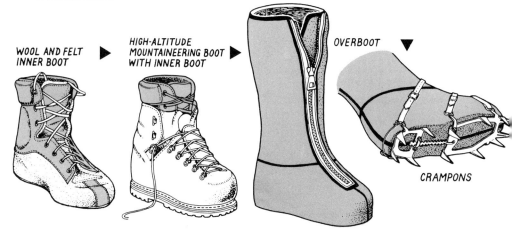

WOOL AND FELT INNER BOOT ▶ HIGH-ALTITUDE MOUNTAINEERING BOOT WITH INNER BOOT ▶ OVERBOOT ▼

CRAMPONS

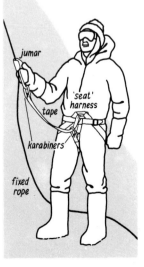

fixed rope

trigger for
releasing rope

toothed plate allows
jumar to slide up rope,
but grips when pulled **down**

hand-grip

karabiner

tape

Out in the early dawn light we look at the foreshortened jumble of grey ice that spreads to the gates of Everest. Breakfast is a silent meal — compo porridge, eggs and bacon forced down on an unwilling stomach purely for their energy value. It is as functional as stoking fuel into a boiler. Back at the tent Philip, the doctor, asks, 'You ready?' 'Ready as I'll ever be.' My first steps feel awkward and uncoordinated, my boot-tips tripping on the rough moraine. The mind is dulled by the cold, the body unfit and complaining. Five minutes from camp and the rubble gives way to glacier: off with our loads while we strap on crampons. From here on it is ice. The next rock across the climbers' path is 7000 feet higher on the Yellow Band of the Lhotse Face.

Red, zip-fronted overboots in stretchy thermal material encase my leather boots. Crampons specially adapted with a broad fitting are attached outside and need to be strapped tightly. (There is nothing worse than applying the front points neatly into steep ice and having the crampons clatter uselessly round one's ankles.) The harness around my waist is adjusted and a length of tape stretches from it like some untrimmed umbilical. Into the tape is clipped the jumar clamp.

Philip is a dark figure in the cold dawn light. He stamps his feet into the gravel and the crampons make a harsh rasping sound. Our loads are lifted on; light ones, hardly more than 20 lb, for this first trip through the Ice Fall. The porters carry double that weight and are already moving swiftly away, a dark column of figures ahead of us.

We move towards the first flag which marks the long, tortuous path through the ice. The air is very still, heavy with frost that turns breath to vapour and bites into my throat. Ahead there is the rhythmic crunch of Philip's footsteps, while below, slumbering comfortably in the early dawn, lies Base Camp.

At first the ice rises gently and the track follows an obvious line up the broad chute of ice, threading through hollows and crossing narrow one-stride cracks in the glacier bed. The first group of climbers up here took four days to work out the safest route, slightly to the left of the main chaos, yet well away from the flank of Everest which is apt to pour its own debris into the Ice Fall. There is a distinct tilt in the slope and the tail of the first fixed rope lies in the crisp snow. To the left is the first deep crevasse like some huge axe wound, four feet across at the top but falling into deep green, infinite emptiness.

Click! The safety rope is secure in the jumar clamp and running smoothly through it as I move forward. The clamp acts like a valve on the flow of rope, allowing progress upwards but biting into the rope if there is any downward pressure. In the old days a climber relied on his companion for safety if the ground below him opened up. Now the safety line, covered in frost and stiff as a fakir's rope, allows a permanent guard.

jumar

'seat'
harness

tape

karabiners

fixed
rope

4   The surrounding ice has become more and more broken; huge blocks teeter against one another, rammed together by the downward slide, steady for the moment, but how long will that last?

Somewhere in the back of my mind is the fact that 34 people have died in this very place, abruptly killed by an unpredictable violence in the ice as Everest shrugged one massive shoulder and dislodged a million tons of debris. Subconsciously I rationalise this gloomy fact. If, for the sake of argument, 50 expeditions have lost 34 people here and each spent two months or 56 days ferrying through the Ice Fall and, say, 50 trips were made daily, then 140 000 actual passages would have been made through this place for the loss of 34. This is probably not much more than some stretches of motorway. Suddenly the ice rumbles and I feel the vibration through the insulation of my boots. Philip hesitates, eyes darting over the sections of ice immediately threatening the track. Then we move on.

I am not yet used to the altitude and it seems unlikely that I ever will become used to it. We are at 19 400 feet, well above any European peak but still well down the Himalayan scale. The air feels thin and biting, drying out and inflaming the skin in my throat. Movement has to be slow and rhythmic; a gentle, purposeful plod, head down and mind in neutral.

Climbers bridge a crevasse near the top of the Ice Fall with ladders. Beyond the huge blocks of ice is the Western Cwm, lying between Everest (left) *and Nuptse.*

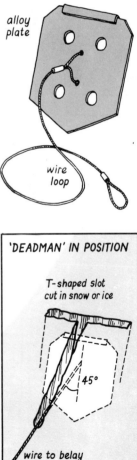

Pumori, one of Everest's smaller neighbours, rises gracefully behind a climber on the Ice Fall. Notice that he is using a fixed rope.

'DEADMAN'

alloy plate

wire loop

'DEADMAN' IN POSITION

T-shaped slot cut in snow or ice

45°

wire to belay

The first bright shaft of sunlight is touching the rocks on Nuptse to the right and the West Ridge of Everest to the left. The famous black pyramid is out of sight, around the corner; below us Base Camp is now no more than a scatter of small bright dots in the curve of the glacier. Sunlight brings beauty and the most blinding brightness to the scene, illuminating the graceful shapes of Pumori and Lingtren, Everest's smaller neighbours. Colour glows from the rocks, snow crystals sparkle and the sky becomes a deep shade of blue. The sunlight spreads down on to us as we reach 'atom bomb alley', a section of the Ice Fall resembling a bowl filled with giant sugar lumps. Safety ropes almost continuously guard this part of the route, switch-backing from one giant block to the next and secured by long metal stakes or the broad blades of 'deadmen' driven into the ice.

Jumar clamp grasped firmly in hand, Dr Philip Horniblow makes his devout way across a yawning crevasse.

Sections of ladder begin to appear, bridging the widest and unavoidable gaps. The porters nonchalantly balance across the rungs, walking upright and murmuring a Bhuddist prayer. Christians adopt the humbler method of crossing the crevasses on all fours, loads tipping awkwardly forwards, rungs rammed uncomfortably into kneecaps.

It is hot now and the sun beats back from the snow. We remove our top padded layers and the clothes underneath steam with condensation. Philip's broad back moves steadily ahead. My goggles are steamed up but without them the brilliant light tears at the retina. Forcing myself back to a steady pace I move on into the broad saucer-like depression of the upper Ice Fall. The opposing walls of Everest and Nuptse are closing in here and squeezing the frozen outpourings of the Western Cwm through a narrow neck.

I understand now why the porters set out so early. The hot sun certainly lights up the savage beauty of Everest but it also soaks up the oxygen, irritates any uncovered patches of skin and turns sweat to a clammy dampness. The porters are already bounding back down the mountain to Base Camp, having delivered their loads at Camp I. The early climber catches the firm snow, it seems, because now the bright sun transforms the top surface of the glacier into a layer of frozen granules which clings to the crampon points and makes progress even more laborious.

The ladders and ropes become a blurred and barely registered succession of physical efforts like the hurdles in some slow steeplechase. Even the final 40-foot span rising from the bed of a crevasse to the lip of an ice platform, into which Camp I has been precariously dug, goes by unremarked.

Camp I perched amongst the chaos of the Ice Fall.

At the camp hot, sweet tea in the largest and most steaming mug I can ever recollect sends a scalding and reviving stream into my system. Next time it will not be so bad, I tell myself. The body slowly adjusts to altitude, blood thickens to make better use of the oxygen available, lungs grow more accustomed to processing thin air. I will become used to the effort. Everest may be higher than anywhere else but the actual scale, I argue, is much the same as any other mountain area. There is Base Camp less than four miles away, little different from the distance between Scafell and the head of Langdale in Cumbria or Snowdon and the Pen-y-Gwryd in North Wales. Be practical, I tell myself, less awestruck. Be like the new generation of mountaineers who come to the Himalayas with the calculating approach of a team of steeplejacks and hammer their way to the top by the most difficult route, present a cryptic description to the mountaineering authorities when they return and then search through the files of the Royal Geographical Society for another goal.

Philip staggers to his feet. 'Home, lad,' he suggests, and we are on our way down the ladders and fixed ropes, with gravity easing the effort. Even so, by the time we stumble into Base Camp two hours later we are exhausted. The porters smile at our tiredness; they have covered the distance between Base and Camp I in half the time we have taken, carrying twice the weight of our loads. 'That's the trouble with having low-altitude lungs,' Philip says. 'You'll get used to it.' I never do.

It is the towering height of Everest which marks it out for climbers. The modern school shies away from the concept of the mountain as a 'challenge', since that particular word smacks too much of stiff-lipped, wholesome effort supposed in some mysterious way to be self-improving. Everest has become a technical problem to be met with a logistical plan. The Ridges have been climbed, the traverse of the West and South East Ridges made and the formidable South West Face defeated.

Porters, laden with stores, ladders and marker-stakes, thread their way up the Ice Fall.

The pile of application forms to climb the mountain grows in the Ministry of Foreign Affairs in Kathmandu. The cost of putting two men on the summit of the world is probably some £100,000, with no guarantee of success, yet even small nations with little history of mountaineering are wanting to try. Already, for example, a Japanese has skied down the Lhotse Face, a group of Indian climbers helped by superb weather conditions has almost sauntered up to the summit, and one member of a team of Japanese ladies has reached the top. All this activity may seem to erode the remote and mysterious quality of Everest, but in fact there are few traces of man there; only the occasional splinter of cane or grotesquely twisted bit of metal ladder thrusting improbably from a crevasse wall, little else. The winds scour the mountain, the monsoon blizzards spread a thick burial-blanket of snow and the ice grinds along its cleansing way, leaving little trace.

The towering face of Nuptse, one wall of the natural cathedral which rises from the Western Cwm.

It is a raw and elemental place. I have rarely felt so snugly cocooned as in the warm folds of my sleeping bag in a tunnel tent almost buried in drifted snow. Inches away the wind screamed wildly through more than 50 degrees of frost. In contrast is the Western Cwm on a calm morning, with the sun slanting on to the 6000-foot wall of Nuptse, washing that vast Face with subtle colour, picking out the complex structure of rock and ice and reflecting in the pigments of crystal like a million cats'-eyes. Ahead in this natural cathedral rises Lhotse, the fourth highest summit in the world, with an altar cloth of glacier tumbling from its serrated summit ridge.

The final 8000-foot wall in the cirque is formed by Everest itself, black and massive against a cobalt sky and with its characteristic plume of cloud streaming from the summit. It is this place which must stop the most calculating technicians in their tracks and force them to consider that there are other reasons for climbing mountains than merely reaching the top.

Colonel Sir George Everest, CB, FRS
Superintendent of the Great Trigonometrical Survey of India, 1823-1843
and Surveyor General of India, 1830-1843.

SURVEY

Peak XV computed

History relates that one day in 1852 Sir Andrew Waugh, Surveyor General of India, was working in his office in Calcutta when a computer — the word had human implications in those days — burst into the room and excitedly announced that he had discovered the highest mountain in the world.

The man had been computing the results of surveys taken months earlier by a party working in the Himalayan foothills on the Trigonometrical Survey of India. They were calculating the heights of the distant peaks. Peak XV lay many miles to the north and only the dark tip of its peak and a faint plume of spindrift was visible among the surrounding giants in the forbidden country of Nepal. Until then Peak IX — Kanchenjunga — had been considered to be, at 28 146 feet, the highest mountain in the world, but here was a new giant nearly 900 feet higher.

Waugh named the peak after his predecessor, Sir George Everest, and it perhaps added to the mountain's fascination that Sir George happened to have a surname which lent such an uncompromising and sublime quality to the highest point on earth. In Tibet the mountain is called *Chomo Lungma* — Goddess Mother of the Mountain Snow, Goddess of the Wind or Goddess Mother of the Land. The Nepalese people call the peak *Sagarmatha* which, translated, has a similar meaning.

It was some years after Everest had been discovered that the heights of the other massive peaks in the 1500-mile Himalayan chain were surveyed and the position of Everest was settled without challenge.

The huge pleat in the earth's surface which forms its greatest mountain range is relatively young in geological terms. Some 50 million years ago, according to the latest theory, one vast slab or plate on the earth's surface collided with another. The more southerly of these plates bore the continents of India and Australia, with the Indian Ocean and a good portion of the South Pacific. This ground into the Eurasian Plate which contained the whole of Europe, central Asia and China. The point of impact was around the Tibetan plateau, part of which was thrust high into the thin air as the invading Indian continent slid beneath it.

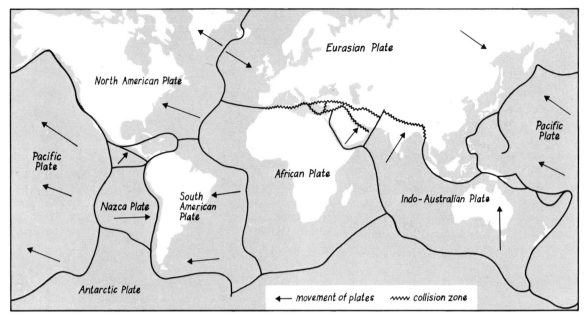

Large slabs of rock, sliced from the Indian continent, littered the new range of mountains. Upthrusts of granite emerged amidst a complex of fold belts, warped and torn by the immense force which created the Himalayas. From the plateau, huge rivers proceeded to drain southward through deeply incised gorges. The Indus, Sutlej and Brahmaputra rivers continued to slice into their two-mile-deep valleys, even as the Himalayas were rearing up implacably around them. During the ponderous time-scale when these upheavals happened, the earth's crust doubled in thickness beneath the High Himalayas and the Pamirs; the high land exposed to the eroding forces of wind and cold became one huge geophysical battleground. Over the succeeding millions of years the peaks and ridges were sharpened by the elements, honed down by vast natural forces to their present chaotic shape.

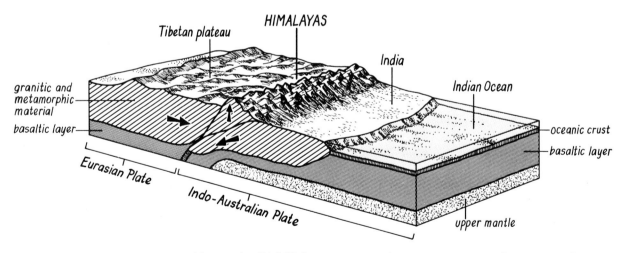

Above the 21 000-foot contour the snow never melts except close to rocks heated by sun. The prevailing wind blowing strongly upon the ridges of the mountain drives the snow and spindrift into a plume which grows solid and may overhang the leeward edge of the mountain by several feet. Such cornices are a major hazard of Himalayan mountains, since the

climber must select a delicate course between the steep and possibly
avalanche-prone weather side of the mountain and the treacherous
cornice.

The snow at these high altitudes falls in an immense volume which
chokes the areas between the ridges: through sheer weight and the effects
of a 100° temperature difference between day and night the snow forms
into ice. The ice, too, becomes fractured by pressure and the relentless
gravitation down the mountain, so that what started life as a feathery
collection of snowflakes ends as a grinding mass of ice which forms
eventually into a glacier.

On steep slopes the snow will form into elegant fluting which builds up
progressively. Each snowfall during calm weather blankets the mountain
uniformly. The sun's warmth releases blocks of snow which sweep down
the furrows whilst the snow on the ridges above hardens. The snow debris
which cascades down the face in avalanches settles at the foot and adds to
the pressure which produces ice; this in turn becomes cold fodder for the
glacier.

The sheer face of Nuptse is scarred by avalanches.

'The perfect crucible for a glacier': in the foreground the Ice Fall cascades from the Western Cwm, which is squeezed between the shoulders of Everest (left) and Nuptse. Behind, at the head of the Cwm, is Lhotse with its hanging glacier.

Everest and its huge neighbours Lhotse (27 890 feet) and Nuptse (25 850 feet) form a classic crucible for a glacier. Their ice-clad walls rise steeply between 6000 and 8000 feet from the flat bed of the Western Cwm, a hanging valley cradled between the three peaks. A constant and massive supply of new ice is forced down into the narrow neck between the shoulders of Everest and Nuptse. From there, in the slowest of motions, the ice descends in a 2000-foot frozen waterfall to the bend leading into the Khumbu Glacier. There it mingles with other debris — large boulders and the gravel of mountain-wall ground down by the abrasive pressure of ice.

When a human element is introduced into this hostile wilderness problems arise. Even at Base Camp on Everest altitude sickness may cause difficulties: high-altitude deterioration is an inevitable and clinically observed process when climbing above 17 000 feet. The effects can be eased but even so are dramatic, with rapid loss of weight and a growing inability to recover from physical exhaustion.

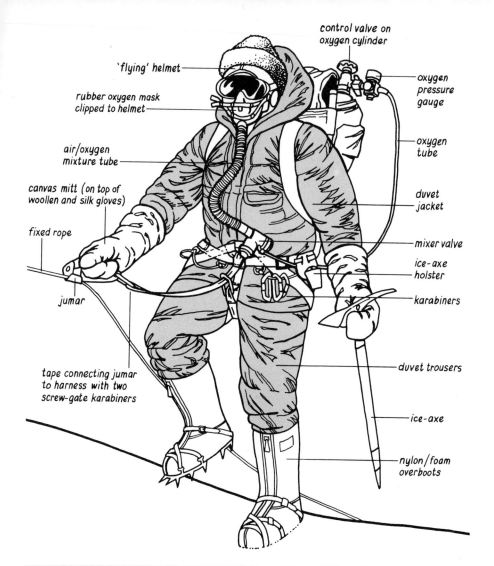

control valve on oxygen cylinder

'flying' helmet

rubber oxygen mask clipped to helmet

air/oxygen mixture tube

canvas mitt (on top of woollen and silk gloves)

fixed rope

jumar

tape connecting jumar to harness with two screw-gate karabiners

oxygen pressure gauge

oxygen tube

duvet jacket

mixer valve

ice-axe holster

karabiners

duvet trousers

ice-axe

nylon/foam overboots

Far left: *Don Whillans*.
Left: *'Brummie' Stokes*.

On the early Everest expeditions the physical stress of living without a normal supply of oxygen was not fully appreciated and was even ignored, which makes the achievement of the climbers much more remarkable. The modern Himalayan mountaineer, with his duvet clothing, specially calculated diet, heavily insulated boots, light and efficient oxygen supply and knowledge of the medical problems involved in high-altitude climbing, is in a different world from the tweed-clad pioneers who had no such benefits. Yet four of these early stoics reached 28 000 feet without oxygen.

Before World War II little progress was made in researching and developing the techniques of high-altitude mountaineering. Part of the problem lay in the feeling which many climbers had that artificial aids should not be used on mountains and that to use oxygen even on Everest was somehow unethical. In addition there was the practical argument that early equipment was so cumbersome and inefficient that the disadvantages heavily outweighed the benefits. It was not until 1952 that scientists fully established that the oxygen-flow rate provided by equipment up to that date had not been great enough to compensate for the weight of the equipment.

The agony of circulation returning to cold hands is clearly seen on the face of 'Bronco' Lane, a member of the 1976 Army Mountaineering Association's expedition. Lane was one of two soldiers who reached the summit.

When diet and fluid intake were properly balanced and climbers were correctly clothed and provided with an ample supply of oxygen, high-altitude mountaineering improved greatly in comfort and scope.

Writing on the medical hazards of high mountains, Dr Michael Ward (who was the doctor on the successful 1953 British expedition) has clearly described the mechanism which makes it impossible for men to live indefinitely at high altitudes because of the combined effects of cold, wind and a depleted supply of oxygen. At any height air contains 80% nitrogen and 20% oxygen. At high altitudes there is a decrease in the pressure exerted by the air of the atmosphere on the earth's surface. On the high reaches of Everest, for example, the atmospheric pressure, and therefore the pressure exerted by oxygen, is only one-third of the sea level value. Normally, atmospheric pressure drives the oxygen from the air, through the lungs and into the blood. In the cells it is converted to energy. However, at high altitude the body must compensate for lack of pressure by increasing both the rate and depth of breathing and the oxygen-carrying capacity of the blood. There is a sharp growth in the number of red blood cells, from about 40% at sea level to 65% at altitude, and the blood makes other adjustments to wrest the maximum use from the available oxygen. Above 17 000 feet the human body deteriorates whether it is working or at rest. Muscle tissue disappears, stamina is sapped and the dry air acts as a rasp on the throat.

The problems do not end there. High altitude demands an increased consumption of liquid, since dehydration is another insidious enemy. Some individuals may require eight pints of liquid each day to keep the physical balance correct.

The horrific effects of severe frostbite: when 'Bronco' Lane and his partner 'Brummie' Stokes had to spend a night out near the summit of Everest, both were badly frostbitten and as a result lost toes and finger-tips.

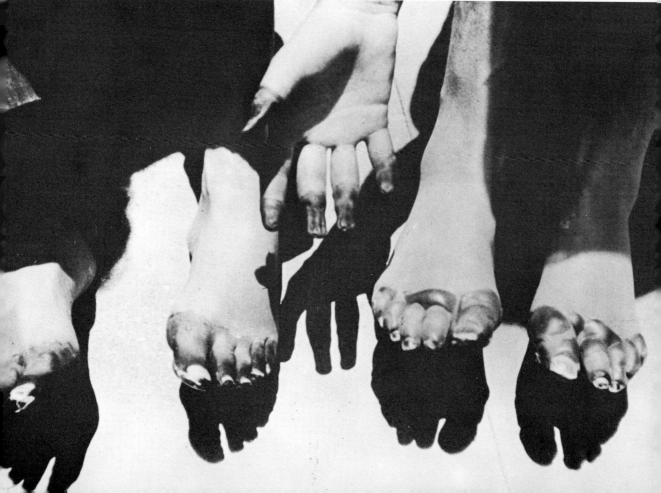

Cold, frostbite, hypothermia and snow blindness are the four high-altitude hazards most easily guarded against, but the psychological pressures of living in a continually hostile and dangerous environment are greater than can be imagined. Whereas an athlete in normal sea level conditions may have a period of strenuous physical activity followed by rest, a mountaineer at great altitudes experiences physical exercise at its most extreme; recovery cannot be complete, the exertion is probably greater and the critical mental balance is harder to maintain. For this reason it is thought that a person in his late 30s or early 40s may have the best natural equipment to withstand the rigours of high-altitude climbing.

The old problem of mountain sickness, first described in 1760, is now known to incorporate a number of distinct clinical symptoms. Cerebral and pulmonary oedema (accumulation of fluid in tissue spaces) may occur with too swift changes in altitude. This explains why the luxurious Everest View hotel above Namche Bazar has a supply of oxygen in every room and medical attendants on hand. Although attacks are less common among mountaineers moving slowly along the Everest approach route than hotel clients just set down from an aeroplane, the complaint is one for which expedition doctors are constantly on guard.

From the aptly-named Everest View hotel, one can just see in the distance the peak of Everest (with its white plume) behind the high Nuptse-Lhotse Ridge. On the right of the picture is Ama Dablam (22 494 ft).

These are the objective dangers which Everest presents. Yet, in spite of the threats to mountaineers from avalanche, cold, exposure, mental disintegration, sore feet, haemorrhoids (piles) and legion other unromantic physical causes, Everest is booked solidly for years to come.

In 1966 Dr Ward wrote that new routes would undoubtedly be attempted on the mountain. He has certainly been proved right. He also said that it was possible that an attempt would be made to climb Everest without oxygen and that a superbly acclimatised mountaineer, given good conditions and good luck, might succeed in this. Again Dr Ward predicted correctly: twenty-five years after the first ascent of Everest, Reinhold Messner, the redoubtable Italian mountaineer, accompanied by Peter Habeler from Austria, achieved just such an ascent.

Dr Ward did wonder, however, whether the qualities for such a feat could not find a more relevant outlet in the exploration of space: 'Scientific knowledge certainly renders the risks unjustifiable and it should satisfy us in this age that men's courage and determination combined with science to break an historic barrier.'

Perhaps Dr Ward misjudged the motivation and determination of the present generation of mountaineers who seek to climb the most difficult mountains by the most difficult route. Messner would answer Dr Ward by pointing out that he is a climber not a rocket pilot. Everest is merely another mountain marginally higher than the rest and technically less difficult than many peaks of smaller stature. The cold, the thin air and the objective dangers, added to the mental and physical demands of reaching the highest peak on earth in a 'pure' ascent without aid, combine to push the threshold of human potential a few attractive steps further.

Reinhold Messner, the first modern mountaineer to achieve a 'pure' ascent of Everest (i.e. without the aid of oxygen).

EARLY ATTEMPTS

In the spirit of the Raj

Everest has always been regarded as a 'British' mountain in the same way that K2 is always associated with Americans and Nanga Parbat with Germans. British climbers took over from where the geographers of the Trigonometrical Survey of India left off. It was a natural perpetuation of the spirit of the Raj that Britain should seek to be first on the summit of the foremost mountain on earth. British climbers were already in the forefront of exploration in the Alps and were beginning to turn their attention to the greater challenges to be found in the Himalayas.

Although Everest had been plotted as the highest point on earth in 1852, political obstacles firmly closed the borders of Nepal and Tibet to any exploration until 1920. Mr Charles Bell, an Indian political officer who had been to Lhasa in Tibet and come to know the Dalai Lama, persuaded the Tibetan government to allow a British expedition through the country to Everest. At the time Nepal was still equally forbidden and mysterious territory.

1921 British exploration party
The Himalayan Committee, formed jointly by the Alpine Club — the doyen of mountaineering societies — and the Royal Geographical Society, began preparations for a British reconnaissance of the mountain. In May 1921 a party of British scientists and climbers, led by Lieutenant Colonel C K Howard-Bury, set out from Darjeeling on the unknown route to Everest, more than 300 miles distant. In the party was George Leigh Mallory who was to become the most famous of the climbers associated with the early attempts on the mountain.

The countryside lying between Everest and the Indian border was

Traversing the deep valleys and rain forests of Sikkim, the 1921 explorers walked along tracks like this.

wild, unmapped and difficult to cross. The party traversed the deep valleys and the rain forests of Sikkim to the broad, 14 000-foot high plateau of Tibet. It was a hard and impressive journey which whetted the explorers' appetites for their first close view of the mountain that formed a stupendous backcloth to the windswept plateau.

George Mallory wrote his first impressions. 'There is no complication for the eye. The highest of the world's mountains, it seems, has to make but a single gesture of magnificence to be lord of all, vast in unchallenged and isolated supremacy.'

As the small party explored the massive, complicated structure of ridges forming the northern approach to Everest, the climbers began to appreciate the objective difficulties which made the Himalayas a challenge apart.

In spite of violent storms and very limited support, after three months of frustrating effort they reached the North Col at 23 000 feet. This was the key to the mountain's North East Ridge. Everest howled and screamed at them as the Himalayan winter approached. The party was prevented from pressing the exploration further but it had been an invaluable visit. The way to Everest was now known; a possible route to the summit had been discovered and much worthwhile material about the mountain and its approaches had been gathered.

The North Face of Everest. The North East Ridge leads to the summit from the left. This was the ridge attempted by the early expeditions, where Norton reached over 28 000 feet and Mallory and Irvine disappeared.

1922 British expedition

Away from the mountain and back in the green-baize gloom of the Alpine Club in London, a full-scale attempt on Everest was planned for the following year. The selection of personnel swung towards a strong climbing team, without benefit of scientists, and this included names which were to become strongly associated with Everest. They were Brigadier General Charles Bruce (leader), Captain Geoffrey Bruce, George Finch, George Mallory, Major H T Morshead, Major E F Norton and Dr T Howard Somervell.

22 Savile Place, London. Original premises of the Alpine Club — the doyen of mountaineering societies.

The expedition was a courageous step into the unknown. There was no record of what might happen to the human body when it was subjected to the physical and mental strain of living at high altitude. No one had climbed higher than 24 000 feet and mountaineers were ignorant about the process of acclimatisation through which a climber gradually adapts to what can strictly be called 'high living'. The planners appreciated that anyone attempting to reach the summit of Everest would have to carry a supply of oxygen (although some of the armchair mandarins of the Alpine Club questioned the ethics of this). The expedition took oxygen equipment which was both heavy and grossly unreliable. Even the climbers whom it was intended to help argued that the weight and cumbersome design of the cylinders would cancel out any benefit.

In March the climbers gathered in Darjeeling and recruited Tibetan and Sherpa porters to transport their stores. (The Sherpas are the inhabitants of eastern Nepal, on the lower slopes of Everest. Many have migrated to Darjeeling in search of jobs and good wages.) By the end of April Base Camp had been set up in the Rongbuk valley and over the next two weeks further camps were established on the broad tongue of the Rongbuk Glacier. The steep rise to the North Col had changed dramatically since the previous year. Instead of a straightforward slope, Mallory discovered a 2000-foot tilted wall of wind-burnished ice.

*Brigadier General
Charles Bruce*

Climbers on the North Col.

On 20 May the route was secured sufficiently for the porters to stock Camp IV on the Col. All was now ready for the team to press on up the mountain into the unknown region. Mallory, Somervell, Norton and Morshead, with a group of porters, set out in freezing conditions and established Camp V at 25 000 feet, an altitude no man had reached before and where some scientists declared none could survive for more than a few hours.

The following day Morshead was weak and frostbitten but the others pressed on laboriously up the mountain. Although they found the actual climbing not particularly difficult, the physical effort was appalling. By early afternoon, when they had reached 27 000 feet, they decided to turn back. At Camp V Morshead was dangerously weak and had to be helped on the way down. Mallory was in the lead when suddenly the rest of the party slid past him. He plunged his ice-axe into the snow, hitched the rope around the shaft and stood by for the shock of the fall. The rope held and the climbers were saved.

The next attempt was made by Finch and Geoffrey Bruce using the crude oxygen sets which the expedition carried. After two nights of ferocious weather at Camp V they set out in calm conditions and, in spite of having spent so long at such an altitude, they reached a commendable 27 300 feet before being forced to give up.

The expedition then retreated for a rest to Base Camp and two weeks later returned for another attempt. However, the monsoon had arrived and fresh snow had massed on the steep ice slopes leading to the North Col. A party taking supplies up to the camp was hit by an avalanche and seven porters were lost. The tragedy ended the attempt.

Everest had shown how brutal high-altitude climbing was, but the expedition had determined that men could survive great altitudes and that the route up the mountain's North East Ridge was feasible. The experience had also shown up the supreme logistics problem involved when climbing Everest. The pyramid of supplies required to put two men on the summit would have to be far greater. Timing, too, was crucial.

George Finch with the primitive oxygen equipment, weighing over 30 lb, which was used by the 1922 expedition.

Dawa Tenzing, now aged 74, who was a porter on the fateful 1924 expedition.

Howard Somervell

Edward Norton

Mallory and Irvine about to leave camp for the final attempt on the summit.

Throughout the winter and spring the massif was continually bombarded by powerful storms and gripped by deep cold which made any movement on the mountain impossible. In the middle of the year the monsoon swept in, bringing with it millions of tons of fresh, avalanche-prone snow.

1924 British expedition

For the next expedition in 1924 all these factors were weighed and it was decided to aim to have as many camps as possible stocked and ready before the period of pre-monsoon calm, so that the best advantage could be taken of the good weather. The party that assembled at the Rongbuk Base Camp included four old Everest hands; Mallory, Somervell, Norton and Geoffrey Bruce. They were full of hope but the mountain turned on them.

A dreadful series of storms demoralised the porters and pinned down the climbers during the days when the route should have been pushed further up the mountain. The temperature sank to 50 degrees below zero, severe winds marooned the various camps and exhausted the climbers without allowing any real progress up the mountain. Tenaciously the climbers stuck to their aim.

On 1 June Mallory and Bruce established Camp V and were then beaten back by the wind. The following day Norton and Somervell with four porters set up Camp VI at 26 800 feet. Next day the weather was perfect — sunshine and no wind — and the summit was little more than 2000 feet above them but looked much closer. Neither man was strong. Somervell was racked by a violent cough which broke the membranes in his throat, filled his mouth with blood and threatened to choke him. Norton was having trouble with his eyes and felt very weak. Throughout the morning the pair moved slowly up the broken overlapping ledges, their nailed boots scraping harshly on the rocks, each step marked by painful breaths. The air remained still and the sun shone quite warmly in mocking contrast to the recent conditions.

By noon they had reached 28 000 feet. Somervell stopped, exhausted. Norton climbed on for another hour, adding a further one hundred feet to the climb. He reached a wide gully separating the North East Ridge from the summit pyramid. His breath rasped painfully in his dry throat; each step was an agony. Infuriatingly the weather was calm, the sky clear, the sun beating down on the summit rocks of Everest. But he could not go on.

Somervell and Norton's achievement without oxygen was a tremendous feat of endurance. Perhaps if they had not been weakened by the appalling earlier conditions they might have succeeded, but Everest is no place for 'ifs'. Had the weather turned on them at 28 000 feet they would not have survived the descent. As it was, Norton went snow blind as they were approaching the North Col.

On 6 June began the most historic attempt on Everest by Mallory and Andrew Irvine, who at 22 years old was the youngest member of the expedition but probably the fittest. Mallory, aged 37, was among the finest mountaineers of his generation, with an impressive record in Britain and the Alps. He was a master at an English public school and a man of dynamic energy who by now had become obsessed by a desire to climb Everest. He had boundless nervous strength and a powerful physique to drive him to that goal. Everest was not to be lightly conquered, however.

The two set out from the North Col, taking oxygen sets with them. Instead of traversing the Face as the previous pair had done they went directly up the spine of the ridge. Soon they were lost from view in mist. Noel Odell, who was in support of them, looked anxiously up the mountain. As the mist momentarily cleared, he caught a glimpse of two tiny figures just below a rock step on the ridge and moving upwards. The mist closed in and the two men were not seen again.

No one will ever know for certain whether Mallory and Irvine reached the summit. The balance of probability must be against their having done so. It is now known that ahead of them was the easy First Step, a small notch on the ridge, and beyond it a thin, broken edge leading to the Second Step at 28 130 feet, an unavoidable 100-foot high rock wall.

The 1924 expedition and its tragic result marked Everest as a peculiarly British battleground. The world was struck by the courage of the mountaineers and by the utter loneliness of their deaths as they pursued a goal for no other reason than, in the words so often accredited to Mallory, 'because it was there'.

Two notes from Mallory to Odell. The first, written at Camp V, commented 'things look hopeful'; the other, reporting 'perfect weather for the job', was Mallory's last message from Camp VI.

FURTHER ATTEMPTS

North and south approaches

The modern Himalayan mountaineer might feel humble when he compares his triple thickness boots, eiderdown clothing, efficient oxygen sets and carefully designed diet with the painfully inadequate equipment used by the early pioneers. There was little serious attempt then to defeat the freezing Himalayan winds. The climbers wore nothing more impenetrable than good tweed, several layers of wool and a thick waterproof top. First World War puttees were useful for keeping snow out of boots but the footwear was more suitable for Snowdon than for the highest point on earth. The achievement of Norton, who reached 28 000 feet, and the remarkable feat of Odell, who spent eleven days above 22 000 feet and twice climbed to 27 000 feet without oxygen, marked the fortitude and determination which characterised these men.

1933 British expedition

After the 1924 expedition Everest remained undisturbed for nine years behind closed borders until, in the autumn of 1932, the Royal Geographical Society obtained permission from the Tibetan government to form an expedition. A new generation of climbers was recruited, under the leadership of Hugh Ruttledge. Among the climbers were men who had already established powerful mountaineering reputations, such as Eric Shipton, Frank Smythe and J L (later Sir Jack) Longland. In March 1933 they set out full of confidence. The party was strong and technically highly competent; equipment had improved. Most reassuring of all was the fact that if Norton and Somervell had been able to reach within a thousand feet of the summit when they were weakened by illness and exhaustion, then surely, granted some luck with the weather, the new expedition would succeed.

Above: *Hugh Ruttledge.* Opposite: *Mallory* (left) *and Norton photographed by Somervell as they approached 27 000 feet, the highest point reached in the 1922 expedition.*

30   They agreed that oxygen should not be used. According to Shipton this decision resulted from a kind of ethical prejudice and a lack of faith in the heavy, cumbersome apparatus then available. The time had not yet come when the extra weight and strain of carrying oxygen equipment was counterbalanced by an improvement in the climbers' performance.

All went well until the third week in May, when Base Camp reported to the camps already set up on the North Col that the monsoon had broken early and was already spreading through the Himalayan foothills. This was alarming news; there was not to be the usual calm spell before the seasonal storm during which a bid for the summit could be made. The weather on the mountain deteriorated but Wager, Wyn Harris and Longland, supported by a group of porters, established Camp VI at 27 400 feet. The heavy monsoon snow began to fall. The overlapping slabs below the summit of Everest, which lay like the tiles on some gigantic roof, were treacherously layered with fresh snow.

Wager and Wyn Harris made the first summit attempt but were unable to climb beyond the gully where Norton had turned back in 1924. Just above Camp VI they found an ice-axe left by either Mallory or Irvine. It may have marked the point where they fell.

Smythe and Shipton, the second assault pair, were pinned down for two nights by a wild snow storm in Camp VI. On 1 June, when they set out for their summit bid, they themselves were weakened and the condition of the mountain had further deteriorated. Shipton moved slowly behind Smythe and eventually suggested that Smythe should go on alone. Shipton wrote later: 'Life at these extreme altitudes is a strange, dreamlike experience. Apart from physical weakness, which makes one feel as though one had just got out of bed after a prolonged illness, the lack of oxygen induces a state of mental torpor that clouds the intellect and numbs emotion. I remember feeling no great sense of frustration or disappointment at being within a mere one thousand feet of the top of Everest and unable to reach it.'

Smythe, having assured himself that Shipton was able to return to Camp VI safely, turned back alone towards the summit, keeping to the crest of the yellow band of rock which lay in smooth slabs deep in powdery snow. He reached the Great Couloir where black overhangs reminded him of a gully on Lliwedd in North Wales. Delicately he made his way across to the foot of the rock buttress on the far side. The holds were choked with snow that was as soft as flour and dangerously loose. With bitterness dulled by altitude, Smythe had to turn back, having reached about the same place as the first summit pair.

Eric Shipton

It was here that he experienced a curious sensation (caused perhaps by weariness, mental stress and lack of oxygen) that someone else was climbing with him. This feeling was strong enough to eliminate all loneliness and it even seemed to Smythe, as he made his solitary way across that dangerous and grossly exposed mountainside, that he was joined by rope to his 'companion', who would hold Smythe if he slipped.

'I remember constantly glancing back over my shoulder and once when after reaching my highest point I stopped and tried to eat some mint cake, I carefully divided it and turned round with one half in my hand. It was almost a shock to find no one to whom to give it.'

The expedition returned defeated.

Flight over Everest

While the climbers on the 1933 expedition were approaching Everest, an attempt was underway to fly two British aircraft over the highest mountain in the world. The aim of this expedition was two-fold: to show that inaccessible country could be surveyed by aerial photography and to prove the technical expertise of Britain's plane-makers and aero-engineers.

When permission was granted to fly over Nepal, the expedition party gathered at an aerodrome at Purnea, northern India, in March 1933. The two pilots were the Marquis of Douglas and Clydesdale and Flight-Lieutenant D F McIntyre, the observers L V S Blacker and S R Bonnett.

On 3 April, in fine weather conditions, both planes — Westlands fitted with Pegasus engines — successfully flew over the summit of Everest. It was only when trying to fly through the plume Everest so often wears, that the airmen discovered it was not in fact a cloud but a maelstrom of ice particles tossed about with great force by a strong north-westerly wind. One cockpit window was broken by the ice.

Because the photographs taken on the flight were not as good as had been hoped, a second flight was made on 19 April. This time the results were better. However, the photographs did not help mountaineers. Viewed from above, mountain features were deceptively flattened or distorted. It was still necessary to explore the Everest approaches on foot.

Opposite
Above: *An ice-axe, grim memorial to Mallory and Irvine, found on the North East Ridge nine years later.*
Below: *A camp site overlooks the forbidden peaks of Tibetan China whose border lies five feet from the tent. Beyond is the curve of the Rongbuk Glacier.*

British expeditions 1934-38

Over the following years the records show that a number of attempts by British parties were repulsed by bad weather. In 1934 a Briton, Maurice Wilson, attempted to climb Everest alone. He died in his tent at 21 300 feet, near the foot of the North Col, after he had refused to return to base with his Sherpa porters. In 1935 an expedition led by Shipton reached the North Col but atrocious snow conditions prevented any attempt on the final pyramid of the mountain. (This expedition found Wilson's body and buried it on the mountain.) The same point was reached in 1936 by a group led by Hugh Ruttledge but an early monsoon again forced retreat. In 1938 the seventh serious British attempt was launched by a small party of climbers led by H W Tilman. Yet again the mountain was blocked by heavy snows. Two pairs of climbers reached around 27 000 feet: Shipton, Smythe and Tilman without oxygen, Peter Lloyd using oxygen.

1947 Canadian, 1951 Danish attempts

World War II concentrated attention elsewhere, then in 1947 a Canadian, Earl Denman, set out on an attempt similar to Maurice Wilson's, accompanied by only two Sherpas. One of the Sherpas was Tenzing Norgay (who was later to become the most famous Sherpa in Everest history, when with Edmund Hillary he reached the summit). The three men reached part of the way up the North Col. The foot of the North Col was also reached in 1951 by a Danish adventurer, K B Larsen.

Everest from the south

The Chinese invasion of Tibet in 1950-51 changed the direction of subsequent Everest attempts, as it closed to western mountaineers the route through the empty land north of the mountain. Nepal, until then a mysterious and unknown country, was jolted into accepting the curious foreigners who sought to climb amongst its highest and most holy sanctuaries.

The possibility of a new approach on the southern side of the mountain had long intrigued mountaineers all over the world. Shipton, after the small expedition in 1935, had already assessed that the southern flank of the mountain would have to be approached through the formidable Ice Fall which was menaced from above by avalanches and was bordered by the 26 000 feet ridge of Nuptse. He gauged the chances of finding a practicable route to the summit from that direction at 30 to 1. He was happy to be proved wrong.

Explorations 1950-51

It was an American explorer Oscar Houston who led the first expedition to this new face of Everest in 1950. With him went Bill Tilman who had been co-leader of an expedition to another Himalayan peak, Nanda Devi, and who had led the 1938 Everest expedition. The party set out from Jogbani, the Indian railhead, and trekked across the foothills of the Himalayas. They reached the Khumbu Glacier but did not have time to penetrate the Ice Fall.

The black triangle of Everest rises behind the West Shoulder (23 000 feet) at left and Nuptse (25 850 feet), centre. Squeezed between these two masses is the Ice Fall which, at far left, flows into the Khumbu Glacier. Moraine borders the stream of ice in the foreground.

Eric Shipton (left) *and Edmund Hillary discuss expedition photographs.*

The following year a group of six climbers, led by Shipton, set out late in the year to explore the upper reaches of the Khumbu Glacier. In the party was a pair of New Zealand climbers, one of whom was Edmund Hillary. The group reached the foot of the Ice Fall and, in order to gain a better view of it, climbed to 20 000 feet on a peak opposite. From there they saw directly into the Western Cwm. Hillary and Shipton realised immediately that the route up Everest from the south was feasible; climbers could thread their way up the chaos of the Ice Fall into the flat plain of the Western Cwm, cross to the Lhotse Face, then follow the dip of the South Col up to the final dark pyramid of the mountain.

The way up the mountain was, in theory at least, now open. Shipton noted a number of advantages about this new approach to the mountain. Although it would certainly be more difficult because of the Ice Fall and the steep Lhotse Face, climbers would have more protection from the prevailing spring gales; also, the tilt of the strata forming the summit made the final ridge less forbidding than the upper part of the North Face.

1952 Swiss expeditions

Through Shipton's tenacious efforts the gateway to Everest was now unbarred. Swiss climbers were the first to exploit this route in 1952. They made two strong attempts at reaching the summit. The springtime assault included nine climbers and several professional guides. They all succeeded in reaching the South Col. From there Raymond Lambert and Tenzing Norgay climbed on to 27300 feet, intending to set up a camp and then return to the South Col. Instead, they decided to stay on at the new camp and attempt the summit the following day. After a bitterly uncomfortable night they struggled on to 27900 feet, then gave up and returned to the South Col. The expedition did not repeat the attempt. The post-monsoon Swiss expedition was also badly affected by severe conditions. The Himalayan winter set in on the mountain and prevented the climbers reaching beyond the South Col. Even in the relative shelter of the Western Cwm the high winds whipped up a maelstrom of ice and snow. The attempt was abandoned. The way was now open for a British attempt which was to become the most famous of all.

Everest viewed from the south west. To the left of the summit the NE Shoulder rests on the ridge rising from the North Col. In the left foreground is the Shoulder from which the West Ridge leads to the summit. The difficult SW Face lies directly below the summit, in the centre of the picture. To the right of the Face is the South Col, the Geneva Spur (the rocky outcrop) and the Lhotse Face with its hanging glacier. The Nuptse-Lhotse Ridge is on the extreme right. Cradled below is the Western Cwm.

CONQUEST

The 1953 expedition

For two years scientists had been working hard to produce warmer, more wind-resistant clothing, and also light and reliable oxygen equipment made from the alloys developed during the war. By 1953, an assault plan was laid for what was to be the eighth major attempt on Everest. Eric Shipton, who had by then been to Everest five times, was a clear choice for leader, but he disliked large, heavily organised expeditions and the sensational publicity which Everest was attracting. He chose as organising secretary John Hunt, an army officer and qualified mountaineer. After some frank discussion Hunt decided that he could accept the job only if he were also deputy leader. Charles Evans had already been nominated for this post. The Himalayan Committee then stepped in to appoint Hunt as co-leader with Shipton. Predictably, Shipton declined the arrangement: he felt that the fundamental differences between himself and Hunt were too great. The Committee then decided to appoint Hunt as leader of the attempt. Shipton, the man who had put so much effort into the conquest of Everest, retired. He admitted that he was neither 'an efficient organiser of complicated projects nor a good leader of cohorts', but his sudden dismissal caused him great sadness.

The whole thrust of the 1953 expedition was based on the use of oxygen while both working and sleeping at and above 23 000 feet. This meant that a heavy pyramid of stores had to be lifted high on to the mountain to ensure that the lead climbers would be well supported should the weather close in and demand siege tactics. By this time doctors knew more about the proper diet for high altitudes; the deterioration which can speedily reduce the human frame to a skeleton at such altitudes is largely due to dehydration from the rapid loss of moisture through the lungs, and can be counteracted by increasing the liquid intake.

The expedition comprised eleven climbers, a physiologist, a photographer, and a reporter, James Morris, from *The Times*. After becoming acclimatised during March while climbing peaks in the Khumbu region, they turned northwards up the glacier to the point where the Ice Fall erupts from the Western Cwm. The tasks of opening the route through the Ice

Opposite: *Entering the Western Cwm with Everest in the background.*
Below: *An expedition member heavily loaded with oxygen and supplies.*

Fall into the Cwm and of stocking the camps below the 4500-foot Lhotse Face took one month. Bad weather pinned down the climbers and it began to look as though the whole attempt would have to be abandoned.

Leader John Hunt (left) *tests the oxygen equipment with which the 1953 expedition conquered Everest.*

Then came the spell of calmer weather which usually precedes the monsoon. On 26 May the first assault was made by Charles Evans and Tom Bourdillon, who set out from a camp on the South Col to cover the 2800 feet to the summit in one direct climb. Edmund Hillary and Tenzing Norgay, selected as the second summit pair, reached the camp on the South Col just as Evans and Bourdillon were preparing to leave. They watched the two men slowly clamber up the final pyramid of the mountain, reaching higher than any man before, and then disappear from view over the South Summit.

Hillary, a man of great drive and competitive spirit, confessed to feeling envy at the fact that Evans and Bourdillon were moving so well, with a clear chance of reaching the top if they could maintain the pace up the final 300 feet. Tenzing, watching beside him, was probably even more concerned and regretful that a Sherpa would not be one of the first

Above: *In the Sola Khumbu, where the expedition undertook preparatory climbs, is this tantalising peak, Ama Dablam (22 494 feet), overlooking Thyangboche monastery. While Evans and others went to explore a suspected hidden valley beneath its southern precipice, Hunt's group inspected the north west face of the mountain.*

Left: *Charles Evans, photographed by Tom Bourdillon, stands on the South Summit of Everest and looks up to the summit itself 300 feet higher.*

climbers to reach the summit of the world. After all, it was the Sherpas who had loyally supported so many expeditions to Everest; very many had died in earlier attempts.

Tenzing (left) and Hillary preparing to set out for the South Col camp.

On the South Col the support party spent an anxious afternoon. Clouds had obscured the summit ridge and the wind had strengthened. Suddenly, about 3.30 pm, the cloud thinned and Evans and Bourdillon could be seen at the head of the Couloir, on their way down. An hour later they approached the camp. With their faces frost-covered, they looked like strangers from another planet. Both were utterly weary. They announced bitterly that they had not been able to reach beyond the South Summit. The descent had been dangerous and at one point they had been lucky to survive a fall in the Great Couloir. Bourdillon, a powerfully built and determined climber, was deeply disappointed that they had not pressed on beyond the South Summit but Evans' mature sense had prevailed. He had been convinced that the climb would have been one-way only: they did not have the physical resources or the time to succeed and survive. In fact the attempt had dangerously drained Bourdillon's tough stamina and the next day he, Evans and John Hunt, together with a Sherpa who had become ill, set off wearily down to Base Camp.

The weather changed; for two nights and a day howling winds and sub-zero temperatures imprisoned everyone in the camp. On the morning of 28 May the wind eased. Lowe, Gregory and a Sherpa called Ang Nyima set out to establish a final camp on the summit ridge. Each carried 40 lb loads. Shortly afterwards, Hillary and Tenzing loaded up their food, equipment and oxygen sets and started off up the mountain, along the trail already broken for them. Although their loads weighed 50 lb each, moving in the footsteps of the others helped to conserve energy and oxygen.

They reached the point from where, in 1952, Lambert and Tenzing had made their attempt on the summit. Only the torn remains of the Swiss tent were left. The group then moved 150 feet higher to where a dump of equipment had been left by Hunt two days earlier, but even this spot was rejected as not being a suitably high enough point from which to launch a summit bid.

The South Summit viewed from the South Col. In the centre of the picture is the gully, the Great Couloir.

Hillary and Tenzing, dressed in their high-altitude gear, approach the site of the final camp,

The party loaded themselves further with the equipment from the dump and pressed on up the ridge. At 27 900 feet they traversed a steep slope to find a secure ledge where the loads were dumped. The support climbers returned down the mountain, leaving Hillary and Tenzing on the ledge. They cut out a wider platform for their small tent, anchoring the guylines with oxygen bottles. The sun set and in the bitter cold the two men feasted off sardines, biscuits, dates, apricots and honey. A shrill whine in the darkness above signalled an intermittent blast of wind which tore at the tent on its precarious ledge.

Hillary and Tenzing on the ledge where they made their final camp.

At 4 am Hillary 'cooked' his solidly frozen boots over the primus to soften them up. Two and a half hours later, after they had drunk several pints of liquid to counter the dangers of dehydration, the pair were ready to set out. Above them, the South East Ridge sparkled in sunlight. Tenzing led off first. When they reached the knife-edge of the ridge the snow was unstable and dangerous. They pressed on to where two oxygen bottles were cached in a hollow. The bottles, left behind by Evans and Bourdillon, contained enough gas to take the climbers back to the South Col.

Committed now to a summit attempt, Hillary and Tenzing were so closely involved with the technical problem of moving across exposed ground, assessing angle and snow condition, measuring time against remaining oxygen and watching for any hints of a dangerous change in the weather, that the dramatic impact of moving towards the highest point on earth could have been lost.

The narrow ridge with its brittle crust led to an impressive snow face below the South Summit. The tracks of the first pair were faintly discernible and showed that they had climbed up rocks on the left and had descended through the snow, thus offering an alternative to Hillary and Tenzing. They chose the snow route. At each step they plunged knee-deep into the soft powder. There was precious little security.

Hillary subdued a feeling of fear, arguing to himself that this was no ordinary mountain. Risks had to be taken. Tenzing too was unhappy about the conditions but neither climber suggested turning back. Taking turns in the lead, they moved slowly, deliberately, up the slope until at 9 am the South Summit was reached. The tension eased.

Ahead lay the crux of the climb; 'impressive but not disheartening' was Hillary's first assessment.

The summit ridge was scoured by the wind. To the right of the ridge, huge finger-like cornices overhung the Kanshung Face. On the windward side, the ridge dropped in a steep snow slope towards the top of a cliff. The Western Cwm lay directly below, 8000 feet away. Hillary selected a line along the snow above the rocks and a safe distance from the dangerously corniced crest. They found the snow there firm and, by skilfully avoiding bumps of ice which blocked the ridge, within an hour they arrived at the foot of the Rock Step which ever since has borne Hillary's name. The Step proved to be quite a problem; a vertical cliff some 40 feet high, bounded on its right by a wall of snow. Between the rock and the ice was a crack which Hillary climbed, congratulating himself on such great effort at that altitude. Tenzing followed sluggishly, but it was now clear that the summit was within their reach. Oxygen consumption was steady, the conditions fine for such a place.

Hillary recalled: 'I had been cutting steps continuously for two hours, and Tenzing, too, was moving very slowly. As I chipped steps around still another corner, I wondered rather dully just how long we could keep it up. Our original zest had now quite gone and it was turning more into a grim struggle. I then realised that the ridge ahead, instead of still monotonously rising, now dropped sharply away, and far below I could see the North Col and the Rongbuk Glacier. I looked upwards to see a narrow snow ridge running up to a snowy summit. A few more whacks of the ice-axe in the firm snow and we stood on top.

A model of Everest and its neighbours showing the route to the summit. In the foreground the Nuptse-Lhotse Ridge casts a shadow over the Western Cwm and the South Col, from where the ascent was made. Clearly visible are the South West Face and the long West Ridge.

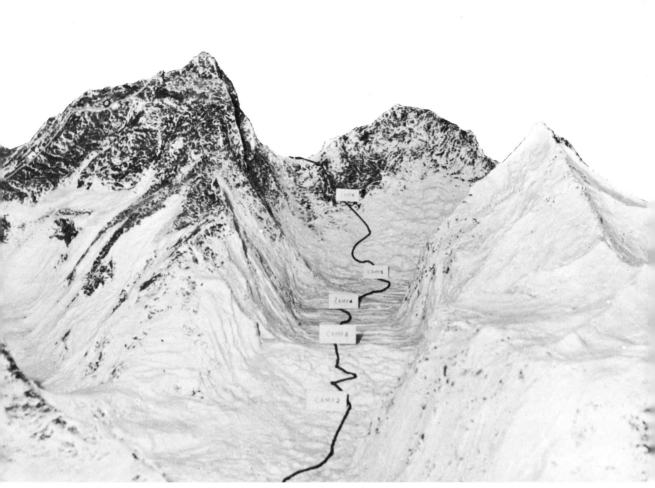

A view of the early stages of the ascent: up the long Western Cwm, round the Geneva Spur (Camp 6) on to the South Col (Camp 7).

'My initial feelings were of relief — relief that there were no more steps to cut, no more ridges to traverse and no more humps to tantalise us with hopes of success. I looked at Tenzing and in spite of the balaclava, goggles and oxygen mask all encrusted with long icicles that concealed his face, there was no disguising his infectious grin of pure delight as he looked all around him. We shook hands and then Tenzing threw his arm around my shoulders and we thumped each other on the back until we were almost breathless. It was 11.30 am. The ridge had taken us two and a half hours, but it seemed like a lifetime. I turned off the oxygen and removed my set. I had carried my camera, loaded with colour film, inside my shirt to keep it warm, so I now produced it and got Tenzing to pose on top for me, waving his axe on which was a string of flags — United Nations, British, Nepalese and Indian. Then I turned my attention to the great stretch of country lying below us in every direction.

'To the east was our giant neighbour Makalu, unexplored and unclimbed, and even on top of Everest the mountaineering instinct was sufficiently strong to cause me to spend some moments conjecturing as to whether a route up that mountain might not exist. Far away across the clouds the great bulk of Kanchenjunga loomed on the horizon. To the west, Cho Oyu, our old adversary from 1952, dominated the scene and we could see the great unexplored ranges of Nepal stretching off into the distance. The most important photograph, I felt, was a shot down the North Ridge, showing the North Col and the old route which had been made famous by the struggles of those great climbers of the 1920s and

Tenzing Norgay on the summit of Everest.

1930s. I had little hope of the results being particularly successful, as I had a lot of difficulty in holding the camera steady in my clumsy gloves, but I felt that they would at least serve as a record. After some ten minutes of this, I realised that I was becoming rather clumsy-fingered and slow-moving, so I quickly replaced my oxygen set and experienced once more the stimulating effect of even a few litres of oxygen. Meanwhile, Tenzing had made a little hole in the snow and in it he placed various small articles of food — a bar of chocolate, a packet of biscuits and a handful of lollies. Small offerings, indeed, but at least a token gift to the Gods that all devout Buddhists believe have their home on this lofty summit. When we were together on the South Col two days before, Hunt had given me a small crucifix which he had asked me to take to the top. I, too, made a hole in the snow and placed the crucifix beside Tenzing's gifts.

Pages 47-49: *How Britain received the news on Coronation morning.*

'I checked our oxygen once again and worked out our endurance. We would have to move fast in order to reach our life-saving reserve below the South Peak. After fifteen minutes we turned to go. We had looked briefly for any signs of Mallory and Irvine, but had seen nothing. We both felt a little tired, for reaction was setting in and we must get off the mountain quickly. I moved down off the summit on to our steps.'

Time was now precious. The steps cut in the ridge made progress less difficult and in an hour they were back on the South Summit. Oxygen was running low and the pair wasted no time, even though the slope below the peak was quite as dangerous as it had been on the ascent. The angle eased and soon they reached the narrow ridge which led to the oxygen dump. Their own bottles were now empty. They clamped on a new supply and continued down to the ridge camp. After a short halt there for a brew of lemon and sugar they moved on, recutting steps in the firm snow of the Couloir, to meet George Lowe who greeted the victorious pair with hot soup and emergency oxygen.

'Well, we knocked the bastard off!' Hillary announced, staggering towards him. Lowe grinned with pleasure. 'Thought you must have,' he said.

The conquest of Everest on 29 May 1953 was the world's most closely guarded secret until a coded message from James Morris to *The Times* reached London. 'Snow conditions bad stop advanced base abandoned yesterday stop awaiting improvement stop all well.' Interpreted, this read: 'Summit of Everest reached 29 May by Hillary and Tenzing.' Her Majesty, Queen Elizabeth was given the news on the eve of her Coronation. Next day the crowds lining the route to Westminster Abbey danced and cheered with delight as the secret from the Sola Khumbu became public property.

Back at South Col camp, the exhausted pair enjoy mugs of hot soup.

NEWS CHRONICLE

No. 33,381   TUESDAY, JUNE 2, 1953   PRICE 1½d.

THE CROWNING GLORY EVEREST IS CLIMBED

THE QUEEN'S DRESS TODAY
Back Page

EVEREST 29,002 FT.   LHOTSE 27,890 FT.   NUPSE 25,680 FT.

NORTH COL   ICE FALL

Tremendous news for the Queen

The new Elizabethan

HILLARY DOES IT

GLORIOUS Coronation Day news! Everest—Everest the unconquerable — has been conquered. And conquered by men of British blood and breed.

The news came late last night that Edmund Hillary and the Sherpa guide, Bhotia Tensing, of Colonel John Hunt's expedition, had climbed to the summit of Earth's highest peak, 29,002 feet high.

New Zealand's deputy premier announced it on Coronation Day ceremony at Wellington —and within seconds it flashed round the world.

Queen Elizabeth the Second, resting on the eve of her crowning, was immediately told that this brightest jewel of courage and endurance had been added to the Crown of British endeavour. It is understood that a message of royal congratulation is being sent to the climbers.

Hillary, a 34-year-old New Zealander, and Bhotia Tensing, 38-year-old leader of the guides and bearers, are said to have made the final 1,000-foot ascent from camp Eight on the upper slopes.

The feat was apparently accomplished on Monday.

A year ago Bhotia Tensing climbed to within 800 feet of the summit with Raymond Lambert, in the unsuccessful Swiss attempt.

NEWS BY RUNNER

The latest news of the progress of the expedition hitherto despatched by runner and received in London yesterday—was that the climbers were ready, as soon as the weather was suitable, to set out from Camp Seven, established high on the South Col at about 26,000 feet, to pitch Camp Eight high up near the summit. Events have overtaken the runners.

Our Walker here reconstructs from the known methods of mountain climbing how the final assault is likely to have been achieved.

The two figures are in wind-proof smocks of different colours, double-lined with nylon, and each wears two hoods beneath the visors the eyes peer out on the roof of the world cliffs, eagles greased against frosting.

Down to the right lies Tibet and to the left Nepal, while death, in a variety of forms, none pleasant, lurks on every side. At such a height no man can survive without extra oxygen. Climbing 26lb. of dead weight, when every ounce can count: but at this stage oxygen must supply what nature will not give. The endurance-time of this oxygen, carried on the back in containers, is estimated at five hours.

Hands are clumsy in three sets of gloves: outer gauntlets of waterproof cotton enclose mittens made of down. Next to the skin, skin tight, are gloves of silk.

It may be necessary for one or other of the men to look after his watch. This is a major decision because of the intense cold, for it will that must be followed by the physical distraction. It can take a minute to carry out.

TEN STEPS A MINUTE

Step by step, in Martian clothing, the two figures move forward, pursuing their race against time and received the conquest of one more metre. Ten steps a minute, no more, could be considered satisfactory: Two hundred feet is what their leader, Colonel Hunt, was hoping for. the estimates roughly tally.

The boots used for so many weeks in the early stages have been discarded. The pairs now worn are not even waterproof

Turn Page Two, Col. 3.

EDMUND HILLARY, whose conquest of Everest sets the seal on the new Elizabethan age, is a 34-year-old bee farmer from New Zealand.

He learned his mountaineering in the Alps of the little Dominion of two million people, and was a pioneer in introducing winter ski-ing there.

He and George Lowe, the other New Zealander of the party, were making a free-lance climb in the Himalayas when Eric Shipton's "look - see" expedition arrived in 1951 to choose a route up Everest.

SMILING, mountain - wise Bhotia Tensing, is the leader of the Sherpa guides and porters who accompanied the expedition.

He is 38 and a veteran of four previous attempts on Everest by the northern route. His Sherpa comrades call him the Tiger.

On May 28 last year Tensing climbed to 28,215 feet with Raymond Lambert of the unsuccessful Swiss expedition before the failure of their oxygen apparatus forced them back.

Tensing's people are a caste of mountain dwellers whose "capital" is Namche Bazar, on the road to Everest. They live by trading with Tibet, Nepal and India.

Prophet Vicky

Yesterday's cartoon from Vicky on holiday.

Malenkov going to the ball

Moscow, Monday. — Mr. Malenkov, Russian Prime Minister, will go to a Coronation ball at the British Embassy in Moscow tomorrow night. With him will be Mr. Molotov, Foreign Minister, and 200 senior officials.

Here the forecast is rain—hail—sun—storm, BUT the crowds are singing in the rain SO—

WHO CARES NOW IF IT SNOWS?

CORONATION DAY FORECAST : Northerly winds, sunny spells, showers with hail and thunder, cold, Mid-day temperature 55 deg.

NEWS CHRONICLE REPORTERS

REPEATED heavy showers lashed the packed campers lining the Royal Way last night. Then the sky cleared and the temperature dropped 13 degrees in a few hours.

But the campers sat it out. And early this morning, cut by a chill wind under the stars, they could still raise a cheer for Britain's Everest victory.

When the news spread, people started shouting : "The new Elizabethans !" Hundreds woke from their blanket beds to dance and sing.

By 1 a.m. 50,000 people were squatting in The Mall. Another 50,000 were camped in Trafalgar Square. Along the route stretched the queue—at a temperature of 45 degrees.

And still they came—from early morning trains at main-line stations, and from 18,000 cars converging on London every hour.

FIRES LIT IN STREETS

People already on the pavements lit fires to keep warm, cooked snacks and tea on spirit stoves, played cards, sang—or tried to sleep.

Earlier, thousands of cheering people surrounded the Queen Mother and Princess Margaret as they drove from Buckingham Palace after spending two hours with the Queen in her private apartments—a last visit before the Coronation.

Reinforced police could not clear a way : the car was halted for 15 minutes beside the Victoria Memorial.

The Queen Mother, in a white feathered gown and off-the-face white hat, and Princess Margaret, in a low-cut smoke-blue gown, waved. Motor-cycle police came to the rescue. But a little later more crowds ran from their pitches and blocked the route to Clarence House.

Fifty thousand people gathered outside Buckingham Palace. Despite the bitter wind, they danced away the hours, sang hymns and popular songs and for hour after hour chanted : "We want the Queen !"

Once the curtains parted above the Palace balcony and a roar went up.

Scotsmen sang "On the bonnie, bonnie banks of Loch Lomond." An elderly man wearing a black homburg hat and carrying a silver-topped cane led hundreds in The Big Apple.

JEWEL GUARD

Outside Westminster Abbey the carpenters, painters and carpet-layers were putting the finishing touches. Six men trimmed and nailed down the plush-blue carpet on which the Queen will step from her coach. Another dashed the last touch of yellow to the Abbey annexe. Two hundred and fifty of them have worked there. Twelve have Coronation seats.

Inside was the Coronation regalia brought earlier in the day from the offices of the Goldsmiths and Silversmiths Company in Regent Street, where it had been prepared for today's ceremony.

The priceless jewels—including St. Edward's Crown and the Imperial State Crown—were laid out on tables in the Jerusalem Chamber, guarded by yeoman warders.

Pictures; Page Five.

Stabbed girl dead in Thames

News Chronicle Reporter

A MURDERED girl was found in the Thames yesterday and last night the police feared her girl companion had been killed too.

The girl in the river was 16-year-old Barbara Songhurst, a chemist's assistant, of Princes Road, Teddington. She was stabbed three times in the back after being assaulted on Lovers' Towpath at Ham, Surrey.

On Sunday Barbara went cycling with her friend, 18-year-old Christina Reed, of Roy Crescent, Hampton Hill.

See Page Five

Flash kills 3 cricketers

Lightning struck three cricketers dead at a Coronation match yesterday. The flash shot through the dressing room at Irlam, near Manchester.

The men killed were Ernest Taylor, 44, Herbert Vaudrey, 37, and George Perry, 31, all of Cadishead.

CENTRAL 5000

WEATHER. — Showers and short sunny intervals. Midday temp 50-55. Sun rises 4.45 a.m., sets 9.10 p.m. Moon 00.13 a.m.-9.34 a.m. Lights 10.07 p.m.-3.49 a.m. tomorrow High water at London Bridge 5.48 a.m.-3.54 p.m

Weather map, Page Two

REST OF THE NEWS

ONE of the greatest footballers of the century, Alex James, died in a London hospital yesterday.

A little man, he always wore long, baggy shorts. The crowd loved that as well as his play. *Alex, by Bernard Joy: Page Five*

Rhee's price

SYNGMAN RHEE, President of South Korea, has stated his terms for accepting United Nations truce terms. He wants a mutual defence pact with America.—*See Page Three*

Pinza favourite

PINZA, Gordon Richards's mount, has overtaken the Queen's colt Aureole as favourite for the Derby. He was 5 to 1 at last night's call-over.— *Captain Heath; Page Nine.*

In other pages—

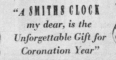

"A SMITHS CLOCK my dear, is the Unforgettable Gift for Coronation Year"

Here is indeed a gift that will be a constant link for years and years to come with this outstanding period in our history. Whether it is for a wedding or a birthday, or a reminder for those 'back home' that British Craftsmanship is still the best ... give Smiths Clocks in Coronation Year!

Sold in a great variety of beautiful models by leading Jewellers everywhere.

ROPER
Handsome Walnut or Mahogany case 8-day clock with four-and-half-hour strike or chime movement. Strike, £8.12.6, Chime, £13.5.0.

SMITHS ENGLISH CLOCKS LTD. · LONDON · N.W.2
The Clock and Watch Division of S. Smith & Sons (England)

DAILY EXPRESS

No. 16,517 TUESDAY JUNE 2 1953 CONTROLLING SHAREHOLDER LORD BEAVERBROOK Weather: Sunny intervals, showers

BE PROUD OF BRITAIN ON THIS DAY, CORONATION DAY

ALL THIS—AND EVEREST TOO

Crowds singing in the rain·

By R. M. MacCOLL

DESPITE the rain, defying the rain, singing in the rain, the People surged into London all day yesterday, and equally sat or lay down in its streets.

They moved in massively on the route of the Procession, with the things they would need for a wait of anything up to 30 hours, and just squatted down.

When it rained, which it did several times, they huddled under oilskins and macintoshes. When the sun came out, they came out.

There was a bit of Bank Holiday on Hampstead Heath about the crowds, a rather dreamlike quality in the sight of women snoozing on the gravel of The Mall pavements in mid-afternoon, and the motor-cars of the great stalled by sightseers.

Three girls made the Queen's dream dress

By BOSS

EXCLUSIVE!

Ron the Daily Express artist, is the only man — apart from designer Norman Hartnell—who has seen the gowns the Queen and the Royal Family wear today. It is from his drawings, and Hartnell's sketches, that the world's Press has now learned the greatest-ever fashion secret.

NOW TURN TO PAGE 3

THE Queen's Coronation dress—simple in style, luxuriant in detail—was made by only three girls. Six girls did the jewelled embroidery.

And when the Queen's dressmaker, Norman Hartnell, was asked to thought of the completed dress he said just this: "I think my little embroideresses have done the finest work of their careers."

The glory of the dress began last October. Hartnell was asked to submit designs.

The dress said the Palace must be both regal and religious. It must have no exaggerated shape because of the robes with which it would be worn.

But it must not be a simple Coronation dress like Queen Victoria's, who was only 18 and unmarried. The Queen could wear something grander.

Said Hartnell: "I sketched numerous ideas and it was only on the eve of presenting them that I had the inspiration.

"It was that the dress should bear the emblems of Great Britain embroidered in full colour."

Her Majesty said she could wear the emblems, but the dress must also include all those of the Commonwealth.

When I first saw the dress on the stand at Hartnell's workroom I got the impression that is was made entirely of glass.

Such is the effect of the thousands of seed pearls each set in its equally small saucer of silver, which entirely cover the white satin bodice and skirt.

The skirt, full and wide to the hem, breaks into full colour on the panels which carry the emblems

BRITON FIR ON ROOF OF THE WOR

Hillary, aged 34, does

Express Staff Reporter

BRITAIN has conquered Ever dramatic message from Colon Hunt, leader of the British Mount Expedition, gave the news last ni the eve of the crowning of Queen E The Queen was told at once.

Edmund Hillary, a 34 - year - old 6ft 4ins. New Zealand bee - keeper, and "Tiger" Tensing, 39 - year - old Nepalese, reached the summit of the 29,002ft. mountain, the highest in the world, on Friday.

They are the first men ever to get to the top of the world — after 32 years of attempts. An Elizabethan performance has thus set the standards for this Elizabethan reign.

And the message they sent from the summit was: "All is well."

Hillary is a bachelor who spends six months a year on his New Zealand honey farm and the other six months climbing the 10,000ft. New Zealand Southern Alps.

"Tiger" Tensing he has this title of honour (tiger) because he has carried a load to 24,000ft.—has succeeded on his eighth Everest trip.

He is a Sherpa, one of a Nepalese people living in the valleys below Everest famed for their hardiness.

The success of Hillary and Tensing has come after a month's battle against the weapons with which Everest has ice treacherous powder snow temperatures dropping to nearly 40 degrees below freezing and winds of 30 to 40 miles an hour driving through windproof clothing

Hacked a way

The triumph is the result of a team effort. The path for Hillary and Tensing was prepared by Wilfred Noyce, 35-year-old Charterhouse schoolmaster, who hacked a way up the steep Lhotse Glacier with the Sherpa Annullu, after all of Noyce's other supporting men had gone down with mountain sickness.

Noyce and Annullu carved steps out of the snow-covered ice and crossed what they modestly called "a very nasty slope over a deep crevasse at the top of the Lhotse Glacier.

They thus made their way to

PAGE TWO, COL. ONE

CEntral t

Daily Mail

FOR QUEEN AND COMMONWEALTH

NO. 17,790 THREE HALFPENCE TUESDAY, JUNE 2, 1953

The GREAT day—and here is news to make it the GREATEST

THE CROWNING GLORY— EVEREST CONQUERED

Edward Hillary plants the Queen's flag on the top of the world

DAWN EDITION

EVEREST is conquered. A Union Jack has flown on the 29,000ft. peak, carried there by a New Zealand bee-keeper. Nature's greatest prize belongs to the Queen this Coronation morning.

This dramatic news from the British expedition reached London last night just as it seemed as if the cruel mountain had once again beaten back its attackers.

Two attempts had failed. The final bid was made by 34-year-old Edward Hillary and the great Sherpa climber Tensing, last Friday, May 29.

From their lonely tent, swept by near gale force winds and with the thermometer at 40deg. below freezing, they had to climb 1,300ft. across rocks, snow, and ice no man has ever climbed.

Each step, each breath, is agony. Even to think is an unbelievable strain.

But they would not be denied—just as Scott of the Antarctic would not be denied. What a triumphant moment it must have been to stand on top of the world, higher than any man has ever climbed before.

They have returned to safety and today Colonel John Hunt, 42-year-old ex-Commando who leads the expedition, has cabled that Everest is tamed at last.

'THIS FORTITUDE A SYMBOL OF THE BRITISH'

Their feat was achieved with only hours to spare. Colonel Hunt always hoped that Everest would be climbed in time for the Coronation. And from the south the monsoon, which could swiftly wipe out the party, was fast approaching.

But the prize had been won, and early today the world rejoiced that the glory had gone to the Queen on the greatest day of her life.

The Premier of New Zealand, Mr. Sidney Holland, spoke in London : "Naturally I am extremely proud that a New Zealand member of this team has been the first...

"What a grand achievement on the eve of the Coronation, and I hope this terrific example of tenacity, the spirit of endurance and fortitude in this, our Coronation year, might be regarded as a symbol that there are no heights or difficulties which the British people cannot overcome."

Sir Winston Churchill at 10, Downing-street was told the news. President Eisenhower at the White House, Colonels cheered in New Delhi clubs. American radio and TV programmes were interrupted for special bulletins.

'I SHALL BE TOO TIRED TO CELEBRATE'

Mrs. Hunt, wife of Colonel Hunt, heard the news at her Llanfihangel, Radnor, home last night. "It's the most...

THE MAN WHO DID IT
He keeps bees

Comment
TUESDAY, JUNE 2, 1953.

A GREATER GLOW

NO Monarch ever rode to Coronation with such splendid tidings as these ringing round her realms.

We have talked and written about a new Elizabethan Age dawning out of the young Queen's reign. The news from the Himalayas is of an epic achievement gloriously in line with the adventurous of the first Elizabethans.

For years past gallant men of many nations have given their energy, skill, and endurance against the pitiful challenge of Everest. That howling top of the world has defied them all till now.

And it is to the Queen's flag and the heroic quality of the Queen's men that Everest has at last submitted.

Superb

THE expedition, though British led and organised, is in personnel an Empire expedition, and the peak has been won by a young New Zealander, accompanied by the intrepid Sherpa Tensing.

We in this island share the pride our kith and kin in New Zealand must feel in their son's splendid accomplishment, for we are of one family, as the great news in London today demonstrates.

Through the vicissitudes of recent years it has been the peculiar virtue of our people that they have not lost faith in themselves or shed their ancient attributes.

Today the whole world sees once more that the spirit to dare and to do within us is as spontaneously as ever. Eyres and Raleigh and Drake brought prizes for their Sovereign from the Spanish Main. Today the conquest of the last unopposed piece of earth is laid at our MAJESTY'S feet.

So the cheers that greet the Queen today will carry with them, for those who hear, an even deeper meaning.

A radiance

1,000,000 LINE THE ROUTE AT FIRST LIGHT

London sees its most amazing scenes

Daily Mail Reporters

LONDON was one vast camp of Coronation sightseers at dawn today. More than 500,000 had spent a wet, wintry night defying heavy rain. Thousands more poured into the procession route with the first trains and buses. Police estimated there were 1,000,000 waiting at first light.

In The Mall, where 100,000 bedded down for the night, police loudspeaker cars at 4 a.m. relayed the order : "All get to your feet."

Men, women, and children obeyed, rubbing the sleep from their eyes. Once on their feet they saw police jump from a fleet of lorries and ask them to hand over stools, folding chairs, and boxes. These were taken to police stations to be claimed later.

THEIR CLOTHES WERE DAMP, BUT THEIR SPIRITS WERE HIGH

At the same time a thousand-strong force of "day-duty police "—from all over the country, immaculate in white gloves and polished boots—took up their positions.

It was the end of a vigil that for many had lasted two nights and a day. Despite the rain and cold wind last night the biggest-ever Coronation crowds began camping out early.

Although their clothes were damp, their makeshift shelters soaked, their spirits were high—and at one minute past midnight in Trafalgar-square became one vast choir.

They sang to the music of buskers' bagpipes, trumpets, and drums, and were led by the voice of one man, magnified through loudspeakers.

The Old Hundredth . . . Land of Hope and Glory . . . Rule Britannia . . . the National Anthem . . . The voices singing these old favourites swept along historic streets, echoed through the subways, and seeped into steamy cafes.

FIREWORKS GO OFF IN PICCADILLY—

A FIRE BLAZES IN THE PARK

The note of pride through it all went higher as the great Coronation Eve news spread through the crowds. Everest has been climbed.

Some paused for cheers. Some sang all the louder. The spirit of pride and gaiety spread through all the Coronation streets. The crowd joined the singing and dancing. Fireworks went off in Piccadilly. A firework blazed in Green Park.

4.30 a.m. LA GIRL MUR HUNT

A photograph showing the route followed by members of the British Everest expedition up the ice-fall (foreground), through the Western Cwm, and thence by the Lhotse face to the South Col (hidden by cloud) and the south-east ridge to the summit.

EVEREST CONQUERED

HILLARY AND TENSING REACH THE SUMMIT

A message was received by The Times last night from the British Mount Everest Expedition, 1953, that E. P. Hillary and the Sherpa Tensing Bhutia reached the summit of the mountain, 29,002ft. high, on May 29. The message added: "All is well."

Thus the British expedition, under its leader, Colonel H. C. J. Hunt, has succeeded in its enterprise. Hillary, a New Zealander, was one of the members of the 1951 expedition which, under the leadership of Eric Shipton, found the Western Cwm and so discovered the southern route to Mount Everest, by which the success of the present expedition was made possible. It was Tensing who, with Raymond Lambert, on the first Swiss expedition of 1952 reached the record height of 28,215ft. on May 28.

If the plans announced were followed, Hillary and Tensing formed the second assault party in this season's attempt. They were using portable oxygen apparatus of the "open circuit" type. The first assault, made on May 25 with "closed circuit" apparatus by Bourdillon and Evans, presumably failed. Both were made from Camp VII—"that vital camp," in the words of our Special Correspondent with the expedition, "established on the bleak plateau on the South Col, at 26,000ft."—and the climbers must have returned safely on the day that they started.

INITIAL FAILURE

The failure of the first assault was not a surprise. The closed-circuit apparatus, in spite of various advantages over the other, was found to have certain definite disadvantages and is, in any case, less well tried. If the second, now successful, attempt had failed, a third was to have been made this season after a 10-day withdrawal to the Western Cwm. Had this in turn failed the arrival of the monsoon

E. P. Hillary

would have necessitated a postponement until the autumn. Plans for this eventuality had been made.

As reported in a message published yesterday, the timing of the assault was delayed, largely through obstacles, caused by bad weather, in the crossing of the difficult ice-covered Lhotse face, which leads to the South Col. This delay led to rumours in Katmandu—whence they were spread abroad—that the pre-monsoon assault had failed. Although there was some sickness among members of the expedition, as well as the obstacle of bad weather, there is no reason to think a withdrawal was contemplated at any stage.

JOINT SPONSORSHIP

The expedition was sponsored jointly by the Royal Geographical Society and the Alpine Club. The members are:—Colonel H. C. J. Hunt (leader), Major C. G. Wylie, W. Noyce, T. D. Bourdillon, A. Gregory, G. C. Band, R. C. Evans, E. P. Hillary, G. Lowe, M. Westmacott, Dr. M. Ward, Dr. L. G. C. Pugh, and T. Stobart.

Plans were made in the greatest detail in London and the expedition was armed with the latest equipment, much of it designed specially for this ascent. The party, most of whose members left England in the first days of February, established its base camp at Thyangboche, in Nepal, on March 26.

There followed a period of acclimatization and training. By mid-April a route was marked out through the ice fall and into the Western Cwm. A camp was set up on the Khumbu Glacier at some 20,000ft. by April 16, when the first tests of the oxygen apparatus were made. At that time May 15 was set as the target date for the assault on the summit.

SUCCESSIVE CAMPS

Plans were made for the establishment of eight successive camps, of which Camp I was the base camp on the glacier, Camp II was half-way up the ice fall leading to the Western Cwm, Camp III at the top of it, and Camp IV the advanced base. Camp V was a stores depôt at the foot of the Lhotse face, Camp VI was half-way up it, and Camp VII was on the South Col at 26,000ft. Camp VIII, perhaps never set up, was to be on the ridge between the Col and the summit.

The tactics of the assault were finally drawn up on about May 14, and the dates fixed for the two attempts were May 23 and 24. Bad weather, with heavy snowfalls, illness among members of the expedition, and a brief moment of reluctance on the part of the Sherpas, many of whom were also ill, conspired to postpone the attack. Because the long journey from the mountain to Katmandu could be covered only by runners on foot, several days had to elapse between the writing of dispatches and their arrival in London. The suspense has been rewarded, if only by the apt timing of the announcement of this great achievement on the eve of the Coronation.

Copyright

LONG RECORD OF ATTEMPTS

fall of Everest, an extraordinary jungle of ice pinnacles and winding ice lanes that has become the staircase to the mountain's summit.

Another major problem of Everest concerns the weather. It is now generally accepted that at only two periods of the year can an assault on Everest reasonably be launched—in the lulls that generally occur in May and September, before and after the monsoon.

Everest has proved so difficult an objective of adventure that the assaults that have been made on it during the past 30 years or so have acquired something of the nature of a campaign; each attempt has been a skirmish in battle rather than a complete battle in itself, and from each climbers have learnt more of the problems of the mountain and of the involved methods that must be adopted to solve them.

The campaign against Everest has fallen into two phases because of the mountain's theatrical situation across the frontiers of two "secret" countries—Tibet and Nepal. Before the last war Nepal was completely forbidden to foreigners, while the Dalai Lama, then the temporal as well as the spiritual ruler of Tibet, was sometimes willing to allow expeditions to Chomolungma, "Goddess Mother of the World," as Everest was known to his subjects.

THE RONGBUK ROUTE

The first seven expeditions to Everest, all British and all between the wars, therefore journeyed to the mountain from the north, starting from Darjeeling and travelling through the plains of southern Tibet to the Rongbuk glacier, which forms the northern highway to the Everest massif. The Lho La pass, high above the moraine hillock on which your Correspondent is sitting, would, if it could ever be crossed, lead a traveller from the south directly into the Rongbuk route of the early Everest adventurers.

The first expedition to Everest, mounted nearly seventy years after the discovery of the mountain as the world's highest, was a reconnaissance led by Colonel C. K. Howard-Bury in 1921. It was saddened by the death of one of its climbers, the celebrated Scottish mountaineer Dr. Kellas, who had a heart attack during the wearing approach march, but its members explored the approaches to Everest from north and east, and found what appeared to be a practicable route as far as the north-east shoulder of the mountain. Next year General C. G. Bruce, working on these findings, led an expedition which made the first assault on the summit. During it G. I. Finch and Captain Geoffrey Bruce climbed to 27,300ft. This expedition, too, was marred by death, for during a later attempt on the summit, just before the monsoon, seven Sherpa porters were killed in an avalanche.

Colonel E. F. Norton led the next expedition, in 1924, made famous and terrible by the disappearance on the high slopes of the mountain of two remarkable Englishmen, George Leigh Mallory and Andrew Irvine. The expedition began badly, with appalling weather. During the early weeks a Gurkha accompanying the party died of a clot in the brain, and a Sherpa porter of frostbite. But in May Norton himself reached a height of 28,126ft., climbing for the last part alone, and early in June Mallory and Irvine set off for a further assault on the summit in high confidence and good weather conditions. They were last seen at about 28,000ft., and it is not known how high they climbed.

AIR SUCCESSES

There were four full-scale expeditions to Everest in the thirties, besides successful flights over the summit made by British pilots flying British aircraft, in 1933. In that same year Hugh Ruttledge led an expedition in the course of which F. S. Smythe, Wyn Harris and L. R. Wager all climbed to about 28,100ft. In 1935 Eric Shipton led a reconnaissance to examine snow conditions and test climbers new to the Himalaya. In 1936 a second expedition led by Ruttledge was thwarted by bad weather, the monsoon arriving in the Everest region exceptionally early, and two years later the last attempt from the north, led by H. W. Tilman, was again defeated by the weather. In 1938 the lull before the monsoon never occurred.

Since the war the pattern of action against Mount Everest has necessarily changed. Entry into Tibet, now under Communist control, is out of the question for western climbers. In Nepal, on the other hand, changes of regime have led to an easing of restrictions on the entry of foreigners. British, French, Swiss, American, German, and Japanese expeditions have all been permitted to enter Nepal in recent years.

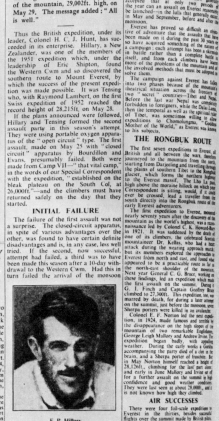

Tensing

The present expedition has enjoyed several advantages over its predecessors, although most of its climbers had little previous experience at very high altitudes—since the war there has not been a large reserve of experienced Himalayan mountaineers in England. First the weather—perhaps the most important and least foreseeable factor of all in an assault on Everest—has not been at its worst: the mountain has shown, in Mallory's words, "forgetfulness for long enough of its more cruel moods." The expedition's oxygen apparatus, after long years of hard trial and sometimes painful error, has proved more satisfactory than before. The Sherpa porters have improved in mountaineering skill and confidence. The *sahibs* enjoyed remarkable good health and fortune in the early weeks of the attempt.

But above all, as Colonel Hunt is first to emphasize, the 1953 expedition has been able to build upon the experience of others. Ten previous expeditions have learnt the lessons of Everest; at least 16 men have died in the learning. To-day, high above the rugged Nuptse ridge, Everest looks as safe, as muscular, as scornfully unattainable as ever; but after 30 years of endeavour the greatest of mountains is defeated, and many the ghosts and men far off who share it

RECEPTION BY

CONTROL OF U.S. FOREIGN AID

THE CHALLENGE OF EVEREST

A BRAVE CHAPTER IN THE STORY OF HUMAN ENDEAVOUR

Seldom since FRANCIS DRAKE brought the Golden Hind to anchor in Plymouth Sound has a British explorer offered to his Sovereign such a tribute of glory as COLONEL JOHN HUNT and his men are able to lay at the feet of QUEEN ELIZABETH for her Coronation day. In spite of the pessimistic rumours that got about last week, it somehow seemed from the outset that the aura of victory went invisibly with this expedition, as with none of the other companies of equally skilled and gallant men who had matched themselves against the giant and fallen back defeated. Nobody could easily give a reason for the air of hope and confidence that surrounded them; but it is pleasant to think that the atmosphere of youth and aspiration belonging to the new reign inspired COLONEL HUNT's men in a contest which, as has long been recognized, could be won only if the spirit repeatedly triumphed over the weakness of the flesh, and even of the exhausted mind.

REPEATED ONSLAUGHTS

For more than thirty years the vast and mysterious challenge of Everest has stirred the imagination of mountaineers, and nerved them to repeated and ever more determined onslaughts. None of these attacks was made in vain. Many valiant climbers whom advancing years have compelled to withdraw from the campaign, or who for other reasons did not have the good fortune to be in the front line at the hour of victory, will hasten to lead the applause for those who attained the goal; but these happy few will be prompt to acknowledge how large a share of honour is the due of the men who opened up the road. All alike will join to pay tribute to the memory of the fellow-adventurers who gave their lives in clearing the way for others—KELLAS, MALLORY, IRVINE, WILSON, and not a few of the Sherpa and Gurkha auxiliaries. The conquest of Everest has been achieved by the cooperative labours and discoveries—and sacrifices—of all the teams who have successively embarked upon the quest.

A REMOTE GIANT

The response to the challenge has been long sustained. It has been a brave chapter in the story of human endeavour. Mallory once said, when asked why men climbed high mountains, "Because they are there." It was he perhaps more than any man who, both before and since his tragic and unexplained death trudging with Irvine on the highest slopes, impressed his spirit of thoughtful gaiety, of patient skill, and of high and most modest endeavour against the mountain. It was almost the last challenge of the unknown and the remote; and it has been finely met.

Everest stands not only geographically but politically remote; the approaches to it, whether from north or south, lie through lands which are always suspicious of visitors from the outside world. Only after the route through Tibet had been closed by Communist revolution did the one through Nepal, by which the summit was eventually reached, happen to become passable. Yet the men who threw themselves so repeatedly against the northern crags made their own contribution to the sum of knowledge. Though their exploration of the Tibetan route was abortive, they painfully accumulated for the benefit of later comers much of the necessary intelligence about the winds and snows at great altitudes, the behaviour of the human body in rarefied atmosphere, and its effect in undermining the power of the will.

The final assault has been accomplished by long and arduous training; by intense study in laboratories of the facts observed in action; by careful study on the part of the climbers themselves of the counsel that science had to give; and by the daily guidance of the specialists accompanying the party. Finally—and to-day this must count above all—it was accomplished by the courage, tenacity, and spirit of comradeship of the men who climbed as one articulated and disciplined unit, though only the small spearhead could even hope to stand upon the summit.

VICTORY OF THE SPIRIT

That spearhead was eventually composed of MR. E. P. HILLARY, a former officer of the New Zealand Air Force who had already won his spurs on Everest, and TENSING, the most famous of the Sherpa porters from Nepal, who had given indispensable service in other Everest expeditions. No two could better represent the qualities which have made the thirty-year old story of Everest an epic. In a sense their glory is unique; nothing can dim the lustre of the memories they will cherish of having stood where no human foot has trodden and seen a view never before seen from the solid earth by human eyes. Yet it is also true that every man in the expedition had his necessary share in bringing the laurels within their reach. To COLONEL HUNT and all his men belongs the fame of this great victory.

That which justifies the expenditure of so much aspiration, effort and even life upon an exploit that brings no visible gain, as gain is understood in the market-place, is the instinctive feeling that these men of valour and resolution are representatives and champions of humanity itself. Their warfare is not against flesh and blood but against the eternal hills, against the mighty pinnacles of lonely rock and snow. Their victory is a victory for the human spirit.

THREE KILLED BY LIGHTNING

CRICKET PAVILION STRUCK

Three cricketers were killed and two seriously injured yesterday evening when, during a thunderstorm, lightning struck the home team's dressing room in the pavilion of the Co-operative Wholesale Society's soap works ground at Irlam, near Manchester. The team was playing against an Irlam district side. Players in the visitors' dressing room were unhurt.

The three killed were Ernest Taylor, aged 44, Herbert Vaudrey, aged 37, and George Perry, aged 31, all married men, and all from Cadishead. The condition of one of the injured, Kenneth John Townsend, of Flixton, was grave.

A flash, which enveloped several of the players, hit the corner of the pavilion where two pedal cycles were leaning. A hole was burned in the side of the building and a short length of wood ripped off. The window on the side where the home team was sheltering was smashed.

Within a few minutes two doctors, police officers, and ambulance men were at the scene. Taylor, Perry, and Vaudrey had apparently been killed instantly. Townsend was unconscious, and for the next two hours doctors, ambulance men, and police worked in relays in the pavilion, using oxygen to save his life. Eventually he partially recovered and was taken to hospital.

Mrs. Hope Robinson, aged 36, of Ilkeston, Derbyshire, was struck by lightning while playing golf at the Chesterfield course yesterday. She was taken to Chesterfield Royal Hospital, suffering from burns on her face and neck.

GALES CHANGE PLANS

Over 50 vessels of the Moray Firth fishing fleet sailed in heavy seas yesterday to take part in a review off Lossiemouth. The gaily bedecked vessels sailed in line astern out of port and past the reviewing vessel H.M.S. Welcome, a fishery cruiser, but so stormy was the sea that it was impossible for the reviewing party to board the cruiser. The ceremony took place from the pier.

What was to have been the chief feature of Llandudno's Coronation celebrations to-day—a fireworks display from the frigate Verulam anchored in the bay—has been cancelled because of a westerly gale. The ship has had to sail to safer waters and 70 officers and ratings are stranded on shore.

A 21-gun royal salute which should have been fired in mid-Mersey from the cruiser Sheffield to-day will now be fired instead in the Gladstone Dock, Liverpool, from the port side of the vessel. High winds last night prevented the cruiser from leaving dock.

STABBED GIRL FOUND DEAD IN THAMES

COMPANION MISSING

Detectives from Scotland Yard last night were investigating the death of Barbara Songhurst, aged 16, of Princes Road, Teddington, Middlesex, who was found stabbed to death in the Thames at Richmond yesterday morning, and also the disappearance of her friend Christine Reed, aged 18, of Roy Crescent, Hampton Hill.

Miss Songhurst, an assistant in a chemist's shop at Richmond, and her companion left Hampton for a cycle ride on Sunday, and were last seen together at Hampton.

Barbara Songhurst's body was found floating near Water Lane, Richmond. There was a wound on her forehead, but it was stated that death was due to three stab wounds in the back. Her shoes were missing.

Close to the towpath, near Teddington lock, and about a mile and a half from the point where the body was recovered, detectives found two pairs of girls' shoes. There was no trace of the bicycles.

Bloodstains on the verge of the towpath near the lock led police to the place they believe the girl was attacked and her body thrown into the river, on the ebb tide some time between ...

NEW ROUTES

International interest grows

The conquest of the highest mountain in the world marked the beginning rather than the end of an era. Other Himalayan giants were 'falling' at about the same time as Everest. Hermann Buhl's solitary ascent to the summit of Nanga Parbat in the 1953 German expedition became one of the most historic mountaineering achievements. The following year K2, the second highest mountain in the world, was climbed by an Italian expedition. Kanchenjunga, at the opposite end of the range, followed in 1955. Since then, explorations have spread to smaller but technically harder Himalayan mountains, although Everest has remained a target for expeditions repeating the South Col route or attempting more demanding variations.

1956 Swiss expedition
In 1956 a Swiss expedition led by Albert Eggler succeeded in reaching the summit by the South Col and added the mountain's southerly neighbour Lhotse to the achievement.

1963 American expedition
The next major accomplishment came in 1963 when a strong American expedition, led by Norman G Dyhrenfurth and with a budget of $405,263, succeeded in traversing the mountain. As one team attempted the South Col route, a second climbed on to the long West Ridge of the mountain.

Base Camp was established on 21 March. On the second day in the Ice Fall, Jake Breitenbach was killed by a collapsing ice cliff. Climbers reached the South Col on 16 April — a month earlier than past expeditions — and on 1 May Jim Whittaker and Nawang Gombu (nephew of Tenzing

Choba Bhamare in the Jugal Himal rises just over the Nepalese frontier in Tibet. Although unlikely to be attempted for many years to come it is obviously a worthy and difficult prize.

Norgay) reached the summit. Meanwhile, on the West Ridge progress was delayed by bad weather; the wind flattened one camp and the climbing party had to retreat.

On 22 May, at 3.30 pm, Barry Bishop and Luther ('Lute') Jerstad were the second pair to reach the summit by the South Col route. Three hours later Willi Unsoeld and Tom Hornbein arrived at the top via the West Ridge — the so-called 'unclimbable' route. They descended towards the South Col, thus traversing the mountain. They met up with the others after dark and spent the night in the open at 28 000 feet. Because of the extreme conditions, all four climbers suffered from severe frostbite and Bishop and Unsoeld later lost their toes.

The achievement of Willi Unsoeld and Tom Hornbein was quite superb. They had reached Camp V at 27 200 feet on 21 May and on the following day had set out on the long and unknown final section of the West Ridge. Almost immediately after leaving camp at 7 am they had trouble with one of Unsoeld's two oxygen bottles. Impatiently, Hornbein suggested that his partner's bottle, which was emitting a steady, disconcerting hiss, did not sound too bad. If the bottle ran out, he said, they could hook up the sleeping tubing and both climb on one bottle. The vision of the two climbers conquering Everest in lockstep, wed by six feet of rubber hose, flitted outrageously through Unsoeld's mind.

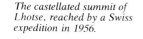

The castellated summit of Lhotse, reached by a Swiss expedition in 1956.

He turned to the climb and led off up a wind-hardened 50 degree slope. They cut a zigzagging line of steps across the first gully, occasionally darting to a patch of rock which made the route seem more secure. It was hard going with the oxygen regulators set at only two litres per minute, half the optimum flow for that altitude. They took turns in the lead and at each 100-foot run-out the first climber pushed his axe into the snow and belayed the second. Between each pitch they turned off the oxygen supply, relying on the ambient air.

The long West Ridge, running from the West Shoulder to the summit.

A steep step of rotten limestone, the so-called Yellow Band, intruded into the ridge. The crumbling flakes of rock held back the two climbers. Six hours after leaving camp they had climbed only 700 feet and Unsoeld's first leaking bottle hissed into silence. They were now above the Yellow Band and beyond the point of no return. Unsoeld reported on the radio to Base that the way ahead was probably easier and that they would be able to move together. There were no rappel points on the cliff to allow a safe return to Camp V: it was 'up and over' for the two of them.

After another 100 feet they reached a steep tongue of snow. It was hard and solid. They planted their crampon points into it and walked, painfully slowly, uphill. A couloir led on to a snow rib which they calculated should lead to the summit snowfield. At 3 pm they had reached the snowfield and decided to traverse back on to the West Ridge across steeply pitched slabs of crumbling shale.

The route they had taken had veered far out on to the North West Face of the mountain. When they regained the West Ridge the South Summit basked in sunshine 150 feet above them. Conditions were fine, apart from a strong wind whipping across the ridge. They were now approaching the eye of that long plume of spindrift which so often adorns the summit of Everest.

They took off their crampons for the next rocky step. Hornbein cast off his first oxygen bottle that had lasted a remarkable ten hours; he immediately felt the relief. With one man climbing, the second belaying him, they moved up the rock on small, 'delectable' holds.

Everest ascent routes.

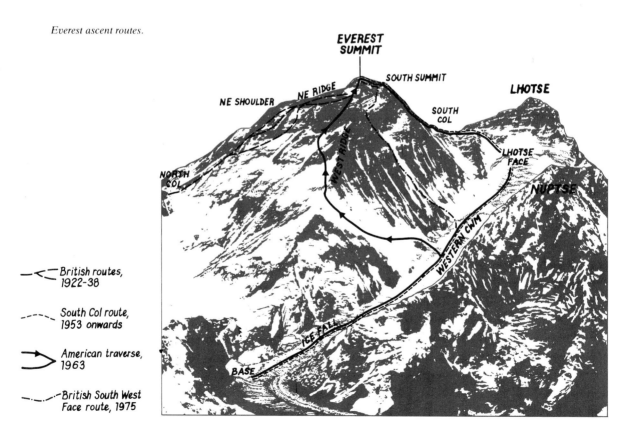

British routes, 1922-38

South Col route, 1953 onwards

American traverse, 1963

British South West Face route, 1975

'The going was a wonderful pleasure, almost like a day in the Rockies. With the sheer drop to the Cwm beneath us, we measured off another four rope-lengths. Solid rock gave way to crud [rotten shale], then snow. A thin, firm, knife-edge of white pointed gently toward the sky. Buffeted by the wind, we laced on our crampons, racing each other with rapidly numbing fingers. It took nearly twenty minutes. Then we were off again, squandering oxygen at three litres per minute since time seemed the shorter commodity at the moment. We moved together, Willi in front. It seemed almost as if we were cheating, using oxygen; we could nearly run this final bit.

'Ahead the North and South Ridges converged to a point. Surely the summit wasn't that near? It must be off behind. Willi stopped. What's he waiting for, I wondered, as I moved to join him. With a feeling of disbelief I looked up. Forty feet ahead, tattered and whipped by the wind, was the flag Jim had left three weeks before. It was 6.15 pm. The sun's rays sheered horizontally across the summit. We hugged each other as tears welled up, ran down across our oxygen masks, and turned to ice.'

Chinese expeditions, 1960, 1969, 1975; Indian expedition, 1960

If on the summit the Americans had discovered a small plaster bust of Chairman Mao Tse-Tung, the Chinese Everest expedition which claimed to have climbed the mountain three years earlier in 1960 would have had a lingering cloud lifted from its alleged achievement. The authenticity of the Chinese victory has always been doubted because of the lack of photographic evidence. Three young Chinese mountaineers, none with more than two years' experience and members of a 214-strong expedition, supposedly climbed the North Ridge of Everest from Tibet (the route used by the early British expeditions) and reached the summit by starlight during the night of 24-25 May. (By coincidence, on 24 May the first Indian Everest expedition of 1960 had established an assault camp at 27 560 feet on the South Col route. The following morning the summit party was forced back by strong wind, blinding spindrift and bitter cold.) A report of the dubious climb, translated from Chinese and published by *The Alpine Journal*, caused quite a furore at the time. Victory was attributed to the leadership of the Communist Party and to the unrivalled superiority of the Socialist system of China without which ordinary workers, peasants and soldiers could never have succeeded in climbing the world's highest peak.

The Chinese were unable to take pictures on the top in darkness but instead offered a photograph taken 'at about 8700 metres' (approx. 28 500 feet) as proof of their ascent. Detailed examination disclosed that the photograph was most likely an enlargement of a frame from a cine film taken some 650 feet lower down. Western climbers, because of the vagueness and the discrepancies in the Chinese account, have tended to discount the 1960 Chinese attempt and have a similarly open mind about the ascent by a survey party nine years later. There can be no doubt, however, about the Chinese expedition which climbed the mountain by the North East Ridge in the spring of 1975. They left behind a 5-foot high metal tripod, anchored firmly to the summit, which remains as a marker.

1962 American attempt

In the spring of 1962 an attempt which Eric Shipton called 'enterprising' and which others have thought highly irresponsible was made by Woodrow Wilson Sayre, grandson of the former American President, and three companions. The group illegally crossed the Nup La from Nepal into Tibet and approached Everest from the north. They reached above the North Col of the mountain before they were bombarded by rockfall and forced to retreat.

1965 Indian expedition

The Indians returned to Everest in 1965 with a large and ambitious team and their persistence was rewarded. Led by M S Kohli, there were nineteen in the climbing team, ten of whom had already been to Everest at least once. During the latter part of May the weather settled into a long spell of fine days and the Indians put a total of nine men in four teams on the summit between 20 and 29 May, using the South Col route. Among them was the Sherpa Nawang Gombu, making his second ascent of the mountain.

1969 Japanese reconnaissance parties

With Tibet and the northern approaches to Everest firmly closed by the Chinese invasion, the West Ridge conquered and the South East Ridge fast becoming the 'yak trail' to the summit, attention focused on the next logical route — up the centre of the South West Face, the highest face on the highest mountain in the world.

British mountaineers had already showed some interest in attempting the Face. The direct route on the Eiger Nordwand had been successfully climbed in 1966, using the kind of advanced techniques and siege tactics that Everest's South West Face would demand. It seemed a natural progression to extend this approach to Everest. However, because of the tender political situation in that part of the world in the mid-sixties, Nepal kept the borders closed for several years until 1969, when a small Japanese group was allowed in to reconnoitre the Face from the Western Cwm. In the autumn of the same year they returned with a stronger team which aimed to reach as high a point as possible on the Face.

From the Western Cwm the south-west flank of Everest rises in a dark-headed pyramid, some nine thousand feet high. A long spear of evenly angled ice runs directly into a huge couloir or open gully blocked by a high wedge-shaped band of rock. Above the formidable cliff stretches a horizontal sweep of slabs then the mountain tilts again to the summit. The Rock Band would clearly be the chief obstacle.

The second Japanese reconnaissance party set up Base Camp on 16 September. Within a fortnight they established a route through the Ice Fall and made Camp II at the foot of the Face. The weather was reasonably settled and there was a good covering of snow on the climb, as near ideal conditions as one could wish for. Their fourth camp at 24 600 feet was pitched near the centre of the gully and the climbers were able to make a closer examination of the route ahead. The gully divided, with one arm on the left curving away towards the West Ridge. Above them a narrow chimney broke the left-hand edge of the Rock Band. To the right a ramp of snow underlined the base of the cliff. Two members of the team, Uemura and Konishi, dug a camp into a bank of hardened snow and the following day two others Nakajima and Satoh, took the climb a further pitch.

The Japanese had achieved their aim. They proved to themselves that their route was feasible by reaching a height of 26 000 feet on the Face. They retreated until the following spring when a large-scale expedition could provide the massive logistics which would be necessary to push safely beyond the Rock Band to the summit.

1970 Japanese expedition

The next expedition was indeed a grand affair with thirty Japanese climbers, nine press and television representatives and 77 Sherpas, a high proportion of these appointed to work at high altitude. The expedition had three objectives; to reach the summit by the South West Face and by the South Col route, and to assist a Japanese ski descent from as high as possible on the mountain — possibly from the South Col. Bearing in mind the experience of the well-recorded American traverse, the Japanese believed that it would be a useful precaution to have the South Col route open and available as a secure line of descent for the South West Face climbers.

The yak trail?

Unfortunately a combination of factors, including the divided aims of the expedition and some appalling ill luck, robbed the Japanese of their main plum, the South West Face.

Eleven days after the climbers started to secure a route through the Ice Fall six Sherpas of the Ski Expedition were killed by an avalanche. A few days later another Sherpa died in the Ice Fall.

At the Western Cwm the strongest team was selected for the South Col route. Included was Naomi Uemura who had been on all the reconnaissance climbs on the South West Face. The ill luck continued. One of the South Col team suffered a sudden heart attack and died; progress on the Face climb was increasingly delayed, partly because of sickness but undoubtedly because there were fewer climbers to press beyond the Rock Band.

On 11 May, however, the redoubtable Uemura and Matsuura climbed to the summit on a fine, still day. The next day a second pair, Hirabayashi and Chotare, a Sherpa, followed their footsteps to the top.

Meanwhile, on the Face the climbers were pursuing the left-hand fork of the snow ramp. They discovered that the snow in fact petered out to give climbing on poor quality rock. From 26 000 feet the route became a rock climb but the days were windless and relatively warm and the climbers were able to progress a further 400 feet to where they could see an easy-looking ramp running left to the West Ridge and a narrow chimney splitting the Rock Band. This route would be difficult, they thought, but not impossible.

As they were descending to the Western Cwm for a rest, one of the Japanese was injured by a falling stone. On the same day another climber was hit by a stonefall. Further attempts were abandoned because the objective dangers could not be justified.

The journalists and film crews went away with a powerful story, however; the only female member of the expedition reached the South Col and the Ski Expedition produced a remarkable film of a Japanese skier hurtling down the side of Everest, only to crash in an explosion of powdered snow when the parachute intended to slow him down failed to open. He was not seriously hurt.

Opposite:
The South West Face.

59

THE HARD WAY

Climbing the South West Face

By 1970 the interest generated by Everest, far from declining as the footprints upon the mountain increased, grew enormously. The waiting list controlled by the Nepalese government ensured that the mountain would be occupied for years to come. The South West Face remained a riddle yet to be solved.

1971 International Everest Expedition

In the spring of 1971 the International Everest Expedition arrived under the joint leadership of Norman Dyhrenfurth, photographer on the Swiss autumn-1952 expedition and organiser of the American traverse of Everest in 1963, and Jimmy Roberts, a retired Lieutenant Colonel in the Gurkhas and a greatly respected figure in Himalayan expedition circles. The primary objective was the direct route of the South West Face with the secondary aim of straightening out the American route on the West Ridge by sticking to the crest of the ridge along its entire length and avoiding a long traverse which the Americans had made in 1963. Altogether the team was smaller and supported by fewer Sherpas than was the Japanese attempt in 1970.

American, British, Japanese, Austrian and West German climbers made up the nine-strong Face team and ten climbers from America, Britain, France, Italy, Switzerland, Norway and India set out on the West Ridge. All went well at first but as the two teams pushed their separate paths up the mountain personal friction between the climbers began to mount. It was, as Don Whillans remarked on his return, 'all prima donnas and no chorus'. The groups included many talented individuals seeking to do well for their own countries and more than a hint of chauvinism undoubtedly crept into the international gathering.

Beyond boot tips on the South West Face, a camp in the Western Cwm, 2000 feet below.

A storm swept the mountain while Wolfgang Axt of Austria and Harsh Bahuguna of India were retreating from their attempt to set up Camp IV on the Ridge route. As Bahuguna lagged behind, exhausted, Axt went on ahead to get help. A rescue party set out and found the Indian where the route traversed a steep slope. He was hanging, in his harness, from a fixed rope. The strong wind blew a wild spindrift of ice particles across the mountain face and darkness was falling. Bahuguna's semi-conscious body was lowered towards easier ground but the rescuers ran out of rope. The casualty swung helplessly. Whillans, unroped, courageously climbed across the slope to him, but he could do nothing. Darkness fell. The storm raged for a further ten days before the climbers were able to recover the body.

Wolfgang Axt (left) *and Harsh Bahuguna checking equipment in the Ice Fall before attempting to reach the West Ridge.*

Considerably weakened, the expedition abandoned the Ridge attempt and concentrated the remaining resources on the South West Face. A virus illness took its toll among the climbers and international tensions added their own strains. Eventually, only Dougal Haston and Don Whillans of Britain, Naomi Uemura and Reizo Ito of Japan, Wolfgang Axt and Leo Schlömmer of Austria and Dr David Peterson of America remained. Whillans and Haston took the lead and established Camp IV at the Rock Band. Instead of following the Japanese (1970) line to the left, the pair traversed right, below the Rock Band, and established a sixth camp at 27 200 feet. To the right lay an easy escape on the South Col Ridge but that would hardly count as a South West Face ascent.

Climbers on fixed ropes about 23 000 feet up the South West Face.

Supplies to the two climbers had dwindled and behind them a bitter row was developing as the Austrians accused the two Britons of hogging the lead. Whillans and Haston said later that they would have been extremely happy to hand on the lead if there had been someone there prepared to take it. From their position far up the Face they had the strong impression that everyone else, apart from the two stoical Japanese and a group of Sherpas, had gone home. Soon the British pair ran out of rope and had to retreat.

Behind all the accusations which filled the air for a brief period afterwards lay the true reasons for failure: a divided objective (repeating the error of the Japanese) and the fierce storm which caused the death of Harsh Bahuguna.

1972 European Everest Expedition

Dr Karl Herrligkoffer

Next came the least happy of all the expeditions so far to the South West Face. It was organised by Dr Karl Herrligkoffer from Munich, whose association with Himalayan mountaineering expeditions had been long and often controversial. He led the first successful attempt on Nanga Parbat in 1953, when Hermann Buhl made his amazing solo bid on the summit. He organised eight other expeditions to that mountain over the following years; three of them on difficult new routes were successful, although Dr Herrligkoffer never took part himself in the lead climbing and generally directed events from Base Camp.

The group which set out for Everest in the spring of 1972 had already survived a wrangle of contractual negotiations and financial troubles long before the mountain was in sight. Originally the expedition was to be called the German-British Everest Expedition, but when seven Austrians, a Swiss, an Italian and a Persian were added to the ten German and three British climbers, it became the European Everest Expedition. The three British members of the team were Don Whillans, who had been on the earlier International attempt, Doug Scott, a powerful mountaineer from Nottingham and noted then for his 'artificial' ascents in Britain and abroad, and Hamish MacInnes, writer and professional climber from Glencoe in Scotland.

Doug Scott (left) *and Don Whillans.*

The team dispensed with the normal acclimatisation period and pressed on rapidly to set up Base Camp at the Khumbu Glacier. Relations within the team quickly deteriorated as the Austro-German contingent demonstrated a strong prejudice against the British trio. Four climbers, Kuen, Huber, Haim and Breitenberger, remained in the lead during the early stages whilst Whillans nursed an outbreak of an old and, for a climber, odd complaint of vertigo and Scott recovered from dysentery. There was trouble too with the Sherpas over the equipment provided for the high-altitude sections of the climb. As the lead climbers tired from the effort of establishing the first three camps on the Face, the climbing leader agreed that the Britons could establish Camp IV provided that they promised not to go any higher on the mountain.

The Khimti Khola near Those, one of the many rivers to cross on the approach route from Kathmandu to Everest.

Time was now moving to the point where the expedition should have been manoeuvring into position for a summit bid. However, the deputy leader recalled the climbers to Base Camp to rest and to greet Dr Herrligkoffer returning by helicopter from Kathmandu. Whillans, concerned that time was running out and keen to use the good weather for climbing, stayed on the Face with the other two Britons, another climber and five Sherpas. They fixed five hundred more feet of rope leading to Camp V, prepared the camp and dumped stores and oxygen there. They descended then to Camp II, where the rest of the expedition was, only to be accused of sabotage for remaining at Camp V for so long. The three Britons continued down to Base Camp, depressed by the outcome of differences between the team members.

On 18 May a summit bid was launched by the Austrians, backed by five Sherpas, but oxygen and other supplies were insufficient for any prolonged assault. Three days later, with the help of the ropes left by the International expedition, Kuen, Huber, Sager and Schneider reached the site of Camp VI on the snow ramp below the right-hand extremity of the Rock Band. As the others put up the tent, Kuen and Huber explored the ground beyond the Rock Band towards the South Col Ridge, the escape route that Whillans had discovered a year earlier.

Chris Bonington

The climbers were prepared to make their bid on the summit on the following day but misfortune struck. The wind built up and lashed their small, crowded tent. The temperature fell. The following morning they had neither the resources nor the stamina to hold out. The attempt was sadly abandoned.

If nothing else, the expedition confirmed that 'meetings of the nations' at such high altitudes do not work; cooperation and trust are of the essence yet are put most severely under strain in these conditions.

1972 British expedition

Into the story now steps a climber who has done more than his share to further British climbing achievements in the Himalayas. Chris Bonington had almost joined the European attempt but decided after discussing the enterprise with Dr Herrligkoffer that success was doubtful. In his opinion the preparations were inadequate and the team too unknown to one another. It proved a wise decision. When an Italian millionaire, Guido Monzino, withdrew his application to climb Everest in the autumn of 1972, Bonington stepped into the vacancy.

His mountaineering record is outstanding. With Ian Clough of Yorkshire he made the first British ascent of the North Wall of the Eiger; with Don Whillans he completed the first ascent of the Central Pillar of Freney on Mont Blanc. He reached the summit of Annapurna II in 1960 on a Joint Services expedition, climbed Nuptse (the third peak of the Everest massif), and led the successful British climb of the South Face of Annapurna I.

The Everest attempt was to be a small-scale assault on the South Col route. However, the South West Face still waited to be climbed after the withdrawal of the Europeans; it would seem very odd to walk up the Western Cwm beneath this ultimate challenge and ignore it. The objective was changed, therefore, even though this meant that the team would have to raise a large amount of extra finance and organise greater logistics in little over two months.

Even more critical would be the post-monsoon weather, when the fine spell yields gradually to the Himalayan winter and Everest becomes impossibly cold and storm-bound. During the autumn the high-altitude winds blow continuously above 24500 feet. This is one reason why the great majority of successful attempts on high mountains have been in the relatively good pre-monsoon weather of April, May and early June.

Bonington gathered together a group of climbers whom he believed would get on well together during the attempt. The obvious choices were Scott, Haston and MacInnes, but surprisingly Whillans was excluded. In all, ten climbers set off after a remarkably swift piece of organisation.

The autumn of 1972 was bad. The cold and the winds produced atrocious conditions on the mountain. By mid-November Haston and Scott reached the point below the Rock Band where they had stopped the previous year, but now the conditions were very different. The upper part of the mountain was doubly barred to them by the Rock Band and a wind which made it impossible to attempt climbing. The climbers retreated and in the very last hours of the expedition a collapse in the Ice Fall killed Tony Tighe, an Australian who had helped the expedition at Base Camp.

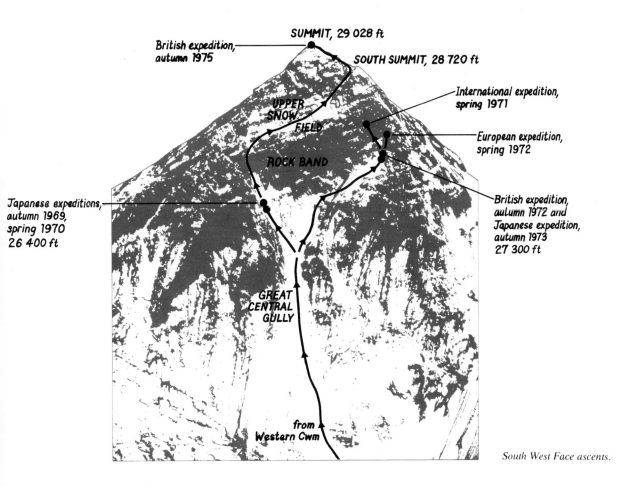

South West Face ascents.

1973 Italian and Japanese expeditions

Five Italians and three Sherpas reached the top in 1973, in a helicopter-supported attempt before the monsoon. In the autumn the Japanese Rock Climbers' Club again reached 26 000 feet on the South West Face before being defeated by storms. One Sherpa was lost in an avalanche. They tried the South Col route next and Ishiguro and Kato reached the summit on 26 October, the first men to conquer Everest after the monsoon.

Women on Everest, 1975

In spring 1975 a member of the Japanese Ladies Expedition, which tackled the South Col route, made history when she became the first woman to reach the summit. Junko Tabei, aged 35, was accompanied by Sherpa Ang Tsering. A few days later, on 27 May, a second woman reached the top via the North East Ridge. Thirty-seven-year-old Phanthog, a Tibetan, was one of nine people on the summit. They were members of the Chinese expedition which planted the metal tripod summit-marker.

1975 British expedition

The next major attempt on the South West Face was made in the autumn of 1975. When a party of Canadians cancelled their expedition, the slot in the waiting list was again taken by Chris Bonington who found the chance irresistible. He also had the good fortune of having a £100,000 sponsorship from Barclays Bank. At the time there were growls in the Press about spending this amount of money during a period of economic cuts. Mountaineers also were critical of such expenditure on a route which would probably prove impossible post-monsoon, or at best would offer only a 50-50 chance of success.

First view of the highest hills on the walk-in to Everest. The summit is lost in the heavy set of cloud.

Early in August the expedition parties were on the long walk-in to Base Camp and by the month's end they had secured the route through the Ice Fall. On 6 September Doug Scott, Mick Burke, a BBC photographer and well-experienced Himalayan climber, Allen Fyffe, a leading Scottish mountaineer and Ronnie Richards, a climber with extensive Alpine experience, set off up the Face. Two weeks later the route was opened to the 1000-foot Rock Band and Nick Estcourt and Paul 'Tut' Braithwaite together found a way up the deep chimney on the left-hand side of the Face. It would have been difficult rock-climbing at sea level but at 27 000 feet in duvet clothing and an oxygen mask the climb was desperate. On the way up Estcourt's oxygen ran out leaving him feeling 'like a 105-year-old war veteran'. At the top of the pitch Braithwaite also ran out of oxygen. He ripped the mask from his face, forced down the sensation of panic and suffocation and scrambled on. Haston and Scott set up Camp VI above the Rock Band on the following day and then went on to fix 1500 feet of fixed rope across the upper snowfield towards the South Summit gully. The way was prepared.

Late afternoon sun warms the bleakness of Camp IV on the South West Face. Sheets of nylon are fixed to deflect powder-snow avalanches.

Doug Scott on the summit. Beside him is the metal tripod left by the Chinese expedition in spring 1975.

At 3 am on 24 September Scott and Haston set off. Struggling through deep, soft snow, they reached the South Summit of Everest at 3 pm. They dug a bivouac hole in the snow before continuing to the final ridge. At 6 pm they watched a magnificent sunset from the summit, where they found the metal tripod and flag left by the Chinese on their pre-monsoon climb that same year. The pair then returned to the South Summit and spent the highest night out in history, suffering only frost-nipped toes and fingers as a result.

They left the bivouac at 6 am and were back at Camp VI (27 300 feet) three hours later. Meanwhile, the second assault party (Mick Burke, Martin Boysen, Peter Boardman and Sherpa Pertemba) were on their way to the summit. Boysen, to his keen disappointment, had to turn back one

hour from camp because his oxygen set failed and a crampon came off.
Burke was moving slowly but Boardman and Pertemba, making good
time, continued to the summit, which they reached at 1.10 pm. On their
return, not far from the top, they met Burke in good spirits on his way to
the summit. They agreed to wait for him at the South Summit. As they
arrived there, the weather suddenly deteriorated, visibility drew in and the
wind strengthened. They waited for over an hour during which time their
condition became critical and they were forced to move down. Feeling
their way along the fixed ropes, they reached the top camp an hour after
dark. Both were in poor shape. Next day the high wind pinned down
everyone, making any search impossible. There was no chance of Mick
Burke still being alive. On 28 September the three climbers made their
way slowly back to Camp V and by 30 September the mountain was
cleared.

The following year when the Army Mountaineering Association
climbed the mountain there was no sign of Mick Burke's body in the
bivouac shelter dug by Scott and Haston. The most likely explanation for
his disappearance is that he fell from the summit ridge in white-out
conditions when the line separating the mountain edge and the 10 000-foot
drop into Tibet would be invisible.

South west from the summit ridge with Nuptse dwarfed in the foreground and a sea of peaks beyond.

'Bronco' Lane (left) *and 'Brummie' Stokes, the two soldiers who reached the summit in 1976.*

1976 Army Mountaineering Association expedition

The expedition in the spring of 1976 was organised jointly by the British and Royal Nepalese armies and marked the first attempt on the mountain by one small club, the AMA, albeit with the backing of two armies and a highly cooperative air force. The climb was the culmination of several years' build-up by the army on other Himalayan peaks. On 16 May two soldiers from the Special Air Service, 'Bronco' Lane and 'Brummie' Stokes, reached the summit. The two men spent a night out without proper bivouac equipment just below the South Summit and both were severely frostbitten.

One aim of the expedition had been for soldiers to undertake much of the high-altitude load carrying and altogether seventeen 'sahibs' reached the South Col. During the ascent, Captain Terry Thompson of the Royal Marines was killed when he fell into a crevasse in the Western Cwm.

Expeditions in 1976 and 1977

In the autumn of 1976 an American expedition repeated the South Col route and reached the summit, thereby celebrating the bicentenary of America. The following spring all eight members of a New Zealand expedition, without assistance from Sherpas, reached the South Col. The strategy followed the modern concept of using a small, compact expedition to attempt even the highest peaks. Without doubt this style of ascent will be repeated.

In the autumn of 1977 a South Korean expedition climbed the South Col route, going from Base Camp to the summit and back in twenty-one days, the fastest ascent ever of the mountain.

Makalu (27 750 feet) viewed from above the South Col. Far away on the horizon lies Kanchenjunga, third highest summit in the world.

Fact or fiction?

The creature has a lumbering gait, red face, size 15 feet and is covered in coarse reddish-brown hair. It has been sighted at least twice and its plate-like footprints have been seen marking the Himalayan snow by at least twenty explorers. The mysterious beast is of course *Homo niveus disgustans*, the Abominable Snowman, known to the Sherpa people as the *Yeti.* He lurks somewhere around the borders of credibility, among the rubble of glacier moraine, the high snowfields and the dense mists of Nepalese fantasy.

Climbers left with little else to talk about during a prolonged Himalayan vigil invariably turn the discussion to the Yeti as the night deepens and the stove-light flickers eerily on tent walls which are being shaken by a supernaturally strong wind. The notion of some lonely missing-link prowling the snows outside adds a touch of marrow-chilling menace to the atmosphere of a high camp: the Sherpas willingly encourage it. Happily, the beast blunders invisibly into conversation more often than he appears in the flesh. It is hard to know what to accept about him. Scientists have tried to evaluate the evidence rationally and to track him down.

Ang Nima, one of my Sherpa friends, has never seen the Yeti but thoroughly believes in him as an animal of prodigious strength and ferocity who eats people. 'Of course he exists; is there not a Yeti skull at Pangboche monastery?' I have seen this particular relic, actually in the smaller monastery at Kunde, the village where Sherpa Tenzing Norgay was born and where the spirit if not the body of the Yeti is very much alive. The skull looked rather like half of a very large coconut and could have been. The local keeper handled it reverently and spoke of it in hushed grunts as he demanded his ten rupees. It is commercialism which more than anything else blurs fact and fantasy. The Sherpas are gentle and polite people who are liable to tell the visitor what he wants to hear. Despairing Sherpa mothers rely on the Yeti as their counterparts in Britain rely on the 'big policeman who is coming to get you if you don't behave'.

Opposite: *The 12-inch footprint photographed by Eric Shipton in 1951.*

Homo niveus disgustans, a rare beast.

The curiosity cult now associated with the Yeti is like that surrounding the monster of Loch Ness, the same narrow margin separating fancy and anthropological possibility — with the added fascination that, if they do exist, both are still alive.

One of the earliest reports of 'Yeti' footprints came on the first reconnaissance of Everest by Howard-Bury in September 1921. At a height of over 20000 feet on the Lhakpa La he saw the print in the snow and ascribed it to a grey wolf. Since then reports of such prints have been the romantic spin-off from many Himalayan expeditions. These reports are rarely first-hand and are more often hearsay.

The story goes that in 1948 two Norwegian prospectors working in the area of the Zemu La in Nepal were confronted with two large, ape-like figures standing upright and answering the description of the legendary Yeti. One man tried to throw a rope around one of the beasts but it bit him and then fled. Other reports titillated the fantasy but there was no concrete evidence until Eric Shipton, the most persistent Everest explorer, produced his famous picture and report of Yeti tracks on the Menlung Glacier in November 1951. The Sherpa who was with Shipton recognised the tracks immediately as those of the Yeti or wild man. The spoor was fresh and had not been affected by melting from the sun. The tracks unquestionably suggested the trail of a biped, walking erect, which ruled out bears and every species of ape or monkey. While these animals would move upright for short stretches, they would invariably drop back on all fours when covering longer distances.

The tracks on the Menlung Glacier photographed by Eric Shipton.

Shipton followed the tracks for almost two miles along the glacier until they led on to the moraine. Some prints were so sharply defined that they must have been made within the previous day. Pad and toe marks were clear within the footprints which were a little more than a foot long. There were scrabble marks on the far side of some of the narrower crevasses which the creature had jumped.

These prints found by Shipton are probably the Yeti's strongest hold on human credibility since they definitely confound the usual explanation of a rolling boulder, a bear, a monkey or a particularly flatfooted peasant being the author of the strange footprints. Certainly Shipton's own scepticism changed to a conviction that there existed a large ape-like creature either quite unknown to science or, at the least, not included in the known fauna of Central Asia. He thought that the evidence of the imprint left by the big toe, which was rounded and projected rather to one side, suggested something quite different from either bears or human beings.

When Everest was climbed in 1953, both Hillary and Tenzing reported finding Yeti prints. Tenzing had grown up with the legend of the Yeti. His father had met one face to face and his description of it was chilling. It looked like a big monkey or ape with deeply sunken eyes and a tall, pointed head. The body was covered in greyish hair and this specimen had large, pendulous breasts which it held in its hands when it ran. Tenzing junior saw no trace of Yeti prints until he was more than 30. However, on the stone slopes and glaciers he had come across droppings, containing traces of rats and worms, that he took to be the dung of the Yeti.

The conquest of Everest revived the old curiosity about the existence of the Abominable Snowman. An expedition sponsored by the *Daily Mail* in 1954 combed the valleys of northern Nepal where the stories of snowmen, if not the snowmen themselves, thrived in profusion. The

The Likhu Khola valley in northern Nepal; could such a valley be the home of the Yeti?

expedition arrived back with some inconclusive droppings. A few hairs plucked from a Yeti scalp also did nothing, when they were analysed, to confirm or deny the existence of an extraordinary animal. At least one other plucking from a similar scalp was despatched for forensic examination and identified as the hairs of a hog. Three expeditions financed and led by wealthy Americans carried the Yeti investigation into the Himalayas in 1957, 1958 and 1959. They had with them X-ray machinery and guns which fired hypodermic pellets but they came no closer to solving the secret of the mysterious beast, although they added a mass of evidence on the Yeti.

Perhaps the realisation that the Yeti, like the mountains, could become financially rewarding accounted for some of the stories and Snowmanabilia at this time. There was an astounding proliferation of Yeti trophies including teeth, dried droppings and fur tufts. Hunting parties were besieged by the entrepreneurs of the Yeti trade who could virtually guarantee a sight of Yeti tracks. How many of these were genuine and how many were produced by inventive gentlemen in massively bandaged feet? The fact and fiction became even more inseparable.

H W Tilman, who is thought to have coined the name *Homo niveus odiosus*, or *disgustans*, became thoroughly convinced by evidence supporting the legend during his Himalayan explorations. The existence of the Yeti was beyond conjecture, he declared. Herdsmen he met in 1949 in the Langtang Himal, some eighty miles west of Everest, confirmed that Abominable Snowmen had recently been in the area and pointed out a cave that they were supposed to have used.

Considering what is now known about the effects of altitude, it is possible that at high altitudes a climber may sense an eerie or even malevolent presence when he is alone. The atmosphere and isolation of the Himalayas may induce a sense of supernatural fear which, linked to the evidence of a footmark or an imprint made by some rational cause, may develop into a snowman sighting.

During 1960-61, Sir Edmund Hillary led an expedition to Nepal to study the physiological adaptation of climbers to high altitudes. Yeti-hunting was added to other secondary aims such as meteorology, glaciology and 'peak-bagging'. The expedition threw a sharp and clinical light on Abominable Snowman theories. Large footprints were dismissed as the remains (enlarged by melting) of old spoor. Skins said to have belonged to the Yeti were proved to have been those of the blue bear. The famous Khumjung scalp, loaned to Hillary and afterwards exhibited in London and New York, was proved by scientists to have been fabricated from the skin of a serow, a somewhat rare Himalayan goat antelope. The Yeti did not survive the pragmatic approach on that occasion. Only the most dedicated Yeti believers continued to argue that the scalp, although a fake, could have been a model of the genuine article, and that behind all the mists of myth there was the solid flesh and bone of the elusive beast.

In the summer of 1970 the Yeti returned to the headlines because of a sighting of footprints reported by Don Whillans, deputy leader of the Annapurna South Face Expedition. In bright moonlight and at a fair distance from his tent he saw a figure bounding on all fours across the crest of a ridge. Whillans believed he was watching some kind of ape-like creature. Earlier that day he had photographed a line of tracks in the snow at 13 000 feet. The depth of snow and the angle at which the photograph is taken make them difficult to interpret, however. Whillans noted with interest the reaction of the Sherpas to the clear and unmistakable footprints. The men ignored the tracks completely. He said later that he was convinced that the Sherpas still had a lurking belief in the Yeti but felt it was best left alone on the basis that if you do not interfere with it, it will not interfere with you. Other sightings by European explorers followed this, but all of the creatures may have been red or black bears or possibly langurs (the long-tailed monkey).

One of the most thorough studies of the Yeti evidence is included in the book *Bigfoot* by John Napier. He concludes after careful sifting of the facts that 'the Yeti of the Himalayas has little going for it. Eye-witness accounts are quite valueless as primary data. Sherpa reports are suspect because Sherpas do not distinguish between the "reality" of the real world and the "reality" of their myth-ridden religious beliefs.' Sightings by western man are, he believes, either fanciful or imprecise because of distance. Footprints are not ultimate proof since the creature which made them clearly varies and where there is uniformity there is the strong hint of a bear about it. Only the Shipton print — clear, crisp, in scale, with its bulbous big toe and pad marks clearly defined — perplexes Mr Napier, who is one of the leading primatologists in the world. 'Without it I would have no hesitation in dismissing the Yeti as a red herring, or, at least, as a red bear. As it is, the issue must lie on the table unresolved.'

Thus the Yeti and the Loch Ness monster and the other unexplained creatures caught between myth and reality are left, if they do exist, to their lonely, elusive lives until perhaps a bone, a shred of skin, a scalp or even a live example proves the fantasy fact. My Sherpa friend would not be surprised. He would merely shrug his shoulders and say, 'I told you so.'

The wavering tracks photographed by Don Whillans in 1970.

NATURE

Flora and fauna of Nepal

The Himalayan Golden Eagle launched herself from a point high on the cliff facing us, her broad wings spread stiffly. For the first few feet of the flight she allowed gravity to build up her air-speed then a graceful turn into the wind brought the huge, predatory shape circling over our heads. An eagle soaring against the backdrop of the Himalayas is a natural and impressive sight. The eyrie was plain to see but quite inaccessible on the cliff; an untidy jumble of sticks with the tell-tale splash marks of droppings on the rock a few feet below.

With menacing grace, the bird remained stiff-winged, delicately balanced on a current of air. Binoculars brought the head momentarily close. Light caught the hard surface of the beak and a hint of retracted talons. We were ignored as the circles above us grew wider. The bird's sleek body caught a strong updraught and curved away to seek more interesting and edible fare. She gave an impatient beat of her wings before disappearing.

Over the next few days we saw other pairs of eagles circling slowly as they hunted near the 9000-foot Deorali Pass, on the walk-in to Everest, and in the Dudh Kosi valley below Namche Bazar. It is true eagle country, because it is towering and majestic. The birds look as natural and proper there as does a robin perched on the handle of a garden spade.

The Lammergeiers are bigger but more rapacious-looking. The largest we saw came close to us, its 10-foot wing span casting a huge and momentary shadow across the path out of Namche Bazar. After a swift appraising glance at us, the evil-faced bird banked away, suddenly a thousand feet higher as it rode upon an uprush of air caused by the strong prevailing wind striking the far side of the gorge. The Lammergeier is commonly called the Bearded Vulture because of the prominent patch of black bristles below the bill and its liking for carrion. A favourite food of the Lammergeier is bones. After vultures have cleaned a carcass — and they do a thorough job — a Lammergeier moves in on the bare skeleton, swallowing small bones whole and dropping larger ones from a great height in order to shatter them into more edible pieces.

A Lammergeier against the Himalayas.

Right: *Alpine Chough.*
Below: *The Dudh Kosi valley, a home of eagles.*

Eagles and Lammergeiers are obvious candidates for observation but the mountaineer bound for his peak can see many more varieties of birds as he makes his way along the beautiful paths through the Himalayan foothills. Our expedition in 1976 spotted some sixty species from Plumbeous Redstarts, courting by a valley stream, to the yellow-billed Alpine Choughs who accompanied the climbers all the way to the South Col. Of course, only a sharp-eyed mountaineer, amidst organising the logistics of an Everest attempt and ensuring a steady flow of food and oxygen bottles up the mountain, would notice that a Rosefinch was sitting on a box of rations in the Western Cwm at 21 800 feet, or that the occasion marked something of an altitude record for Rosefinches. The field guide by Salim Ali suggests that the birds rarely rise higher than 10 000 feet in summer. Exactly which of the four sub-species our specimen was, we had no time to discover. After the briefest appearance it flew away in the direction of the Ice Fall.

Few countries can offer such a variety of plant, animal and bird life in one border area as does Nepal. The walk through the foothills is made memorable by the wild tangles of rhododendron bushes full of brilliant colour and quite often accompanied by different varieties of orchid. There is also a rich assortment of bright alpines each adding its own splash of colour to the grazing grounds below 14 000 feet. In the lower mountain areas vegetation consists mainly of a mixture of larch, oak, pine, poplar, rhododendron and walnut. Between 10 000 and 12 000 feet birch trees are mingled with fir. Other large forests are of cypress and juniper.

Rhododendrons line the footpath to Everest.

A large proportion of Nepal's 10·8 million population lives in the fertile Kathmandu valley and in the intensely cultivated hills to the north. There the pressure of agriculture has removed any unusual plant or animal life but a little further south towards the Indian border the other face of Nepal may be observed. The Terai, in contrast to the cold and barren wastes of the Greater Himalayas, is the home of tiger, leopard, rhinoceros and elephant. The countryside is tropical jungle — hot and steaming in summer — where the animals are wild and malaria is endemic.

The Terai is being opened up as a tourist area and Tiger Tops Jungle Lodge is little less than an hour's flight from Kathmandu by light plane. Guide books give gaur (a wild ox), buffalo, bear and several species of deer

The intensely cultivated Kathmandu valley.

A meadow at Pheriche (13 900 feet), lying below the peaks of Kantaiga I and II.

as native to this area. The deer include the Chital or Axis Deer and the large coarse-haired Asiatic Deer. The muddy, fast-flowing rivers abound with crocodile. The Lesser Rapti Valley in the Chitawan district is said to be one of the last homes of the great Indian Rhinoceros (*Rhinoceros Unicornis*). About half the surviving numbers live in Nepal. The species suffered badly at the hands of poachers as its horn, powdered, was reputed to be a powerful aphrodisiac.

From the excellent vantage-point of an elephant's back, the visitor at Tiger Tops may enjoy the organised tours. In the jungle the presence of an elephant, albeit with a curious hump on its back, does not arouse any sense of menace. The native wildlife will graze serenely as the lumbering tourist-carrier moves past. Similarly the elephant is unperturbed by the close proximity of leopards, snakes and rhino, but it may stop in its tracks and trumpet with fright when a jungle chicken crosses its path. Although the jungles of Nepal do not offer the variety and abundance of wildlife to be found in an African game park, they do have an immense amount of interest and colour and there is no sense of over-exploitation.

Opposite: *The tiger, at home in southern Nepal in the area called the Terai.*

The Chital or Axis Deer, content to graze pasture or browse among the trees, adapts to both marsh and jungle.

Opposite: *Two beautifully marked Hog Deer.*
Right: *A slumbering gavial (or gharial) crocodile, whose diet is fish. Though just as fearsome to look at as other crocodiles, this species is no danger to man.*

Right: *A fine specimen of Indian Rhinoceros, for once without its attendant mynah birds who feed on the rhino's parasites and on the insects it disturbs when on the move.*
Below: *The long and the short of the Nepalese leech.*

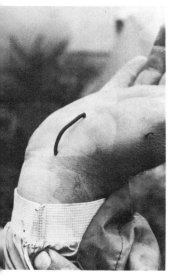

Most mountaineers have more to think about than flora and fauna during an expedition; it is not a lack of interest, simply concentration on the job in hand. If a rare alpine plant is uprooted to provide a handhold, or some sensitive species is disturbed in its nest, then so be it.

In Nepal, however, the fauna — in the shape of the Nepalese leech — can retaliate most ably. Particularly after the monsoon, the leeches lurk behind every bush and grass-blade, awaiting the passage of richly blooded limbs to latch on to. The leeches are either black or brown, about an inch long and with a sucker at each end. No aperture in one's clothing is too small for them to penetrate. They hide their presence on one's body with a nip of local anaesthetic which dulls the pain as they suck blood. A leech will feed contentedly for more than a day if it remains undiscovered. When at last it falls to the ground, gorged with blood, it leaves behind a nasty open wound.

The beautiful blue Himalayan Poppy, which grows in meadows and screes at 13-17 000 feet, has a secret weapon; sharp spines on its leaves and stem which discourage foraging animals.

To try to remove a feeding leech by plucking it away with the fingers is to invite having the second sucker, which is quite as voracious as the first, fixed to the finger. The leech, which is as sociable as the Yeti is shy, can be repelled by paraffin, brine or dry salt. Boots with sewn-in tongues or puttees may also give protection. H W Tilman recalled the 'robust fellows' who soon satisfied themselves that there was no nutriment in leather and so advanced rapidly up the trousers. In heavily infested areas up to fifty leeches could all be climbing at once and a fast mopping-up operation was necessary. Some travellers have been known to put up mosquito nets to ward off the leeches at night. The Sherpa people appear to have developed some degree of immunity to leech attack. Although they are often bare-legged and bare-footed the leeches tend to ignore them and to concentrate on non-orientals.

Even the leeches cannot detract from the great beauty of the ridges and the deep valleys which border the Himalayas. At certain altitudes there are meadows similar to a British mountain pasture containing sedges, vetches, buttercups and chickweed. Within a short space it is possible to move from these into thick forests of fir with bamboo undergrowth. The ornithologist exploring the most barren, scree-ridden areas will generally have something to look at or listen to. The shrill chirrup of the tiny Nepal Wren will remind him that there is life even in this wilderness.

A swing in the foothills above the Bhota Kosi valley.

NEPAL

People and politics

Mountaineers owe a great debt to the people of Nepal, particularly to the Sherpa folk of the Sola Khumbu who have given so much of their energy, and sometimes their lives, to help parties of all nationalities to climb the lofty and remote peaks of their country. The people are materially very poor but tough. They remain remarkably cheerful considering the hardship of their everyday life. Their country has few metalled roads; everything has to be carried along the interminable, steep tracks which are soundly worn into the hillsides. The tracks are centuries old and always take the most careful and economical line. A sturdy Sherpa will invariably out-carry the average expedition member because he is used firstly to the altitude and secondly to the discomfort of a 60 lb load which moulds more naturally on to his back. The hardy and indomitably cheerful women will happily carry 40 lb all day without difficulty and for less than £1.

The classic walk-in from Lamosangu, on the main road which runs between Lhasa in Tibet and Kathmandu in Nepal, gives a fascinating view of Nepalese village life. This walk eastwards across the high ridges which spread in long, green fingers from the Himalayas is now an increasingly popular tourist trek. Large, western travel organisations offer walks from Kathmandu to the feet of the Himalayan giants and firms with such quaint names as 'Yeti Travel' and 'Third Eye Tours' will organise a group excursion into the mountains.

It is savagely beautiful countryside, rich in colour and interest. A constant stream of foot traffic passes along the winding tracks. At most wayside halts there are large vessels from which chang is poured, a sharp-tasting liquid which the Nepalese drink as beer. The western stranger is warmly welcomed in houses where the style of life has not changed for centuries. Some villages have as a centrepiece a massive banyan tree spreading out its huge and shady arms across the huddle of mud- and rock-walled houses with their thatched roofs. The steep hills around the villages are intensively terraced; every patch of the countryside seems to have been put to productive use in the hills and valleys before the Lamjura Pass, where the more rugged Sherpa country begins.

Opposite: *The peaks of the Jugal Himal.*

A ladder for Everest; the hardy Sherpa women at work.

A banyan tree spreads its shady arms over a huddle of houses.

For many years Nepal was a closed country, little known and self-exiled from the rest of the world. It is perhaps the sensitive political position that Nepal now holds between India and China which has prompted the country to shuffle a little closer to the modern materialistic world; however it remains one of the last absolute monarchies where political parties are banned.

Diplomatic observers speak admiringly of the way in which the Nepalese government performs a balancing act between the surrounding massive powers and succeeds in winning aid from a great variety of countries. A new road running east-west across the country, 'from nowhere to nowhere' as one Nepali put it, has been built in sections by several different countries each contributing a large sum of money. The Chinese have added the north-south road linking Lhasa with Kathmandu and have provided an electric bus service in the city. China, India, New Zealand, Switzerland and Norway have all provided substantial assistance and Britain maintains the Gurkha regiment. It is possible that Nepal receives money from more sources than any other country in the world, yet it remains one of the poorest, with a gross national product of about $90 a year per head (although in some remote areas money is not used at all).

The country is 500 miles long and 100 miles deep and occupies about one-third of the Himalayan range. There are thousands of majestic peaks along the north border but the government's 'permitted' list includes only about thirty which are open to mountaineering expeditions. Everest and its immediate neighbours are among them.

In the days of the early attempts on the mountain everything had to be portered overland from India. Now there is a road to Kathmandu and an international airport which allows American tourists on package tours into the Nepalese capital to stay at comfortable hotels, take treks into the foothills and on fine days fly by light aircraft around the Everest basin.

In contrast to the high northern valleys where rivers such as the Dudh Kosi, fed by the melt water of the Khumbu Glacier, flow down from the Himalayas, is a long, narrow strip of jungle called the Terai which borders

Approach route scrapbook: Opposite, top: A hill homestead high above the Sun Kosi river. Beyond are the high peaks of the Jugal Himal.
Below left: Young Sherpa girl.
Below right: The main street of Those, an iron-smelting settlement on the Khimti Khola river.

Above: *A primitive plough churns the foothills near Bhandar.*

Right: *The approach route to Everest threads for 250 miles across the cultivated ridges that run down from the Himalayas.*

upon India and is rich in tropical animal life. The Terai used to provide some of the world's finest big game shooting. When King George V spent a week there as the guest of Maharajah Chandra Sham Shev, his personal bag included 21 tiger, 10 rhinoceros and 2 bear. Hunting is now greatly restricted, but sight-seeing safaris are encouraged.

Around Kathmandu is a broad and fertile valley which is intensively though primitively cultivated. The city itself is very old and its extremely busy maze of narrow streets has changed little from the twelfth century. Ancient temples with ferocious statues guarding them shelter the occasional hippy. Kathmandu was a renowned destination for the hippy community until the coronation of King Birendra in 1975, when the selling of cannabis and other drugs was officially banned.

Outside the city area the standard of life falls rapidly. Health figures show that only half of those born live to the age of 5 and life expectancy is 45 years. Where medical aid has infiltrated the remote areas, the population has grown, countering any improvement in the wealth of the country. With its present resources Nepal cannot afford to feed more mouths. It is a tragic position, shared by other 'third world' countries, whereby if the death rate at birth were improved or the average life span increased, then even more people would suffer starvation. Although there is no religious objection to birth-control in Nepal, education is difficult: in areas where people do not seek medical aid for a broken leg, there is little chance of their seeking family-planning advice. In a land where medical care has still not defeated tuberculosis as an endemic disease, the authorities can hardly be expected to concentrate on more sophisticated medical programmes.

Green eyes of the gods at Kathmandu . . .

Buffalo carts in the Terai.

While development of villages in the Terai is providing an outlet for the congestion in the Kathmandu valley, outside observers fear that Nepal now subsists upon a critical knife-edge and could eventually face ecological disaster. One reason for this is that the country's timber, the only readily available source of heat and energy, is being consumed at a prodigious rate. Hillsides once shrouded in woodland have been stripped of cover and in some places left barren. The rich top soil, unprotected from monsoon floods and strong winter winds, is turned to silt in the powerful rivers which flow from the Himalayas. Much cultivation has been lost because of this but the country remains, perhaps ironically, one of the few food-exporting countries of Asia.

Observers feel that urgent action is now necessary to protect the future. Such action would take the form of hydro-electric schemes — Nepal has more potential as a source of this form of power than the whole of North America put together — and an emergency tree-planting programme. A first step would be to stop selling the timber, which has taken a hundred years to grow, for only a few pence per bundle. However, the poor folk of the highlands would then rightly demand to know how they could be expected to cook food and keep out the cold; any further drift of population towards the Kathmandu valley would only make the country's problems worse.

Since everything except food has to be imported into land-locked Nepal, prices are high. Most of the imported goods arrive through the Indian sea port of Calcutta and so Nepal relies heavily upon good relations with India. In 1974, according to a government report, imports valued at $20 million entered Nepal but the bureaucratic inefficiency of the transport system between the two countries was such that Nepal had to pay $12 million in storage charges before the goods could be distributed.

In addition to the imports problem there is the constant political pressure resulting from being a buffer state between two larger neighbours who have no love for one another. India, with its effective control of Nepal's imports, has expressed dislike of the 'undemocratic' way Nepal is run. The Nepalese reply is that India has enough problems already without launching an offensive on Nepal and that such action would in any case antagonise China. Relations between the three neighbours are therefore delicately balanced, with Nepal following a policy of impartial diplomacy.

99

Overleaf: *Sherpa porters at ease. An evening meal is prepared by the pathside.*

An old Sherpani rests beside her yak.

Above: *Prayer wall in Khumbu.*
Right: *Horns and symbols at a puja ceremony at Thyangboche monastery. The gods are asked to bless an expedition — for a fee.*

Across the Lamjura Pass, into Sherpa country, the land is steeper,
more rocky and less cultivated. Life is therefore that much harder but
curiously the people are much more cheerful. As they are of Tibetan stock
the Sherpas are Buddhists. Buddhism spread across the border and the
religion is reflected in a more kindly attitude to life and a cheerful
acceptance of the hardships which remoteness and a harsh, unyielding
countryside impose. Sir Edmund Hillary has shown his gratitude towards
the Sherpa people by organising several projects, providing schools and air
strips, which have given life in these remote valleys a better future and
greater security. Trekking parties and mountaineering expeditions have
also brought a rich source of income to the Sherpas.

Thyangboche monastery (12 700 feet) set on a wooded ridge above the Imja Khola river.

Namche Bazar is the capital of the Sherpa country and is built on a hillside overlooked by a line of ferociously towering peaks. The approach to it is along a steep track bordered by fir trees, juniper shrubs, rhododendrons and tenacious patches of pasture where small cattle graze. All the houses are made on the same plan, south-facing with handsome wood carving ornamenting the doors and window shutters. On the ground floor are the winter stables for the yaks or other animals. A staircase leads up to the main living-quarters where a fire burns constantly. As there are no chimneys the smoke collects in the roof beams; this ensures that the thatched roof is pest-free but acrid smoke hanging about the living room causes eye infections, one of the chief complaints in this part of Nepal.

On one side of the room is the family altar, a sculptured recess above a low couch. Before a group of silver-framed Buddhas, reminiscent of Russian icons, are placed the usual offerings of lustral water rice, a butter lamp and a prayer book, made of hand-printed paper sheets, which is carefully wrapped in silk squares.

A visitor to the house, with eyes streaming from the captive smoke billowing out of the fireplace, sits on a bench by the window and accepts a porcelain bowl containing chang. The alternative is buttered tea. The Sherpas make this by boiling a brick of coarse Chinese tea, with salt and a pinch of soda, for twenty minutes. The liquid is then churned thoroughly with fresh butter and the result to a western palate is usually not pleasant. Mixing the tea with roasted barley flour produces tsampa, the bread of central Asia.

Outside, beyond windows which totally fail to hold back the keen evening frost, daylight dies on the peaks opposite Namche Bazar, turning the fluted snow crimson. The firelight flickers within the room, lighting up the swarthy, weather-beaten faces of the Sherpa family who are the hosts. More chang is ladelled out to everyone, even to the toddler sitting on a blanket in the corner. On the far side of the room the fire's flames are reflected in large copper pots and pans hanging on the wall.

Sonam, the man of the house, is to be the Sirdar (the chief Sherpa) on the coming expedition. He will select the men who will act as the high-altitude porters. As more chang is drunk the atmosphere grows even friendlier and soon everyone in the room is singing and dancing. Sonam pulls out a fiddle-shaped instrument which he plays by pressing the base against his stomach. The night wears on, the dancing becomes wilder and the men of Namche celebrate the start of yet another expedition to the highest point of the world which lies just beyond their village.

Namche Bazar, capital of the Sherpa country.

Glossary

Acclimatisation The slow process by which a body adjusts to living at high altitudes. Basically the blood stream develops more red corpuscles in order to make more efficient use of the lower levels of oxygen caused by lower atmospheric pressure.

Altitude sickness Caused by the failure of the body to acclimatise to high altitudes. Symptoms are headache, chest pains and swelling in face and limbs, requiring treatment with oxygen and immediate evacuation to a lower altitude.

Belay A safe halt during a climb. *To belay* is to tie oneself to a projection of rock or, in the case of a snow and ice climb, to an ice-axe or deadman (*q.v.*).

Bivouac To make a temporary (overnight) shelter, by digging a snow cave or rigging improvised cover, to escape the cold and wind.

Chimney A narrow, vertical crack in rock or ice.

Col A high pass or saddle; a depression in a high ridge. On Everest the *North Col* and *South Col* are famous landmarks, from which the North and South Ridges lead to the summit.

Cornice An overhanging mass of snow formed along the lee side of a ridge by prevailing winds.

Couloir A large funnel-shaped gully; often a natural chute for stones and avalanches.

Crampons Steel frames, with spikes, which are strapped to a climber's boots to give grip on ice or snow.

Crevasse A fissure in a glacier.

Cwm An enclosed valley. The *Western Cwm* on Everest was so called by George Mallory after the cwms of north Wales (*cwm* being the Welsh form of *coomb*).

Deadman A metal plate which is dug into snow or ice to provide a belay (*q.v.*) point. Attached to the plate is a loop of wire to which the climber's rope is fixed. When the deadman is correctly placed, any force on it tends to drive it deeper into the snow, thereby providing a safe hold.

Fixed rope Lengths of nylon rope fixed by a lead climber to deadmen (*q.v.*) or snow stakes on difficult or threatened sections of the mountain. Each climber following this roped route attaches a jumar (*q.v.*) clamp to the rope. This allows him to move up the mountain safely and at his own speed.

Frostbite The effect of exposing skin to intense cold. Circulation to

107

extremities, particularly fingers, toes, nose and ears, is cut off by the lower temperature and the flesh is deadened. Unless circulation is restored quickly the flesh dies. In extreme cases amputation is necessary to prevent the spread of gangrene.

Glacier A river of ice, formed from the great weight of hardened snow gathered in the high valleys (also called cirques or cwms), which grinds its way to lower altitudes where it eventually feeds the river system.

Ice Fall A 'frozen waterfall' created when a glacier (*q.v.*) tumbles over a steep drop (as, on Everest, the 2000-foot fall from the Western Cwm to the Khumbu Glacier). Because of its constant slow movement, an ice fall is usually an unstable jumble of deeply crevassed ice that is highly dangerous.

Jumar A metal clamp into which a fixed rope (*q.v.*) is fitted. The clamp, which is attached by tape to the climber's harness, slides freely along the rope as the climber moves up the slope but if downward drag is placed on the clamp the mechanism bites into the rope, thus holding the climber securely.

Moraine Rocks and debris strewn on the surface or at the sides or 'snout' of a glacier.

Pitch One section of a climb. A pitch extends from one belay (*q.v.*) to the next.

Rappel To descend by means of a doubled rope or a fixed rope (*q.v.*) anchored on a belay (*q.v.*). *Abseil* is the German term for the same procedure.

Rock Band A point at which a horizontal layer of rock breaks out into the surface of the mountain side (as, on Everest, the 1000-foot rock wall across the South West Face).

Run-out The length of rope used in one particular section of a climb.

Snow blindness A painful condition caused when the eyes are left unprotected from the bright glare of the sun reflecting on snow.

White-out A condition caused by mist, when the sky and the snow become indistinguishable and when the horizon melts into a featureless white haze.

Bibliography

Everest: the early expeditions

C K Howard-Bury, *Mount Everest: The Reconnaissance, 1921*
    (Edward Arnold, 1922)
E F Norton, *The Fight for Everest, 1924* (Edward Arnold, 1925)
W H Tilman, *Mount Everest, 1938* (Cambridge University Press, 1938)
J Hunt, *The Ascent of Everest* (Hodder & Stoughton, 1953)
R Izzard, *The Innocent on Everest* (Hodder & Stoughton, 1954)
J Morris, *Coronation Everest* (Faber & Faber, 1953)
W H Murray, *The Story of Everest* (Dent, 1953)
E Hillary, *High Adventure* (Hodder & Stoughton, 1956)

Everest: the later expeditions

T Hornbein, *Everest: The West Ridge*
    (Sierra Club & Ballantine Books, 1968)
C Bonington, *Everest South West Face* (Hodder & Stoughton, 1973)
C Bonington, *Everest The Hard Way* (Hodder & Stoughton, 1976)
J Fleming & R Faux, *Soldiers on Everest* (HMSO, 1977)

Mountains and mountaineering

M Ward (ed.), *The Mountaineer's Companion*
    (Eyre & Spottiswoode, 1966)
E Shipton (ed.), *Mountain Conquest* (Cassell, 1965)
E Shipton, *That Untravelled World* (Hodder & Stoughton, 1969)
M Milne (ed.), *The Book of Modern Mountaineering*
    (Arthur Barker, 1968)
J Cleare, *Mountains* (Macmillan, 1975)
C Clarke, M Ward, E Williams (eds), *Mountain Medicine and Physiology;*
    proceedings of a symposium for mountaineers, expedition doctors and
    physiologists (Alpine Club, 1975)

Miscellaneous

J Napier, *Bigfoot* (Cape, 1972; Abacus/Sphere Books, 1976)
Salim Ali, *Indian Hill Birds* (Oxford University Press, 1949)
The Story of the Earth (HMSO, 1972)

Acknowledgments

The author and publisher make grateful acknowledgment to the following for the use of material:

Photographs

Alpine Club (photos. John Cleare) for pages 23, 27, 30 (top).
Ardea, London for pages 80, 82 (top), 86, 87, 88 (1 & 2), 89, 98.
Associated Newspapers Group Ltd for pages 47, 48.
Peter Barwell for pages 35, 53.
Beaverbrook Newspapers Ltd for page 48.
Chris Bonington for page 66.
John Cleare/Mountain Camera for pages (iv), (x-xi), (xii), (xiv), 2, 4, 9, 20, 32-3, 39 (top), 50, 60, 62, 63, 65, 77, 84, 91, 92, 94 (all), 96 (top), 97, 99, 100-1, 102 (top), 103, 104.
Crown copyright. The plates on pages 15 (right), 16, 30, 36, 59, 73 (from *Soldiers on Everest*, HMSO, 1977) are reproduced with the permission of the Controller of Her Majesty's Stationery Office.
HTV Cymru/Wales (photo. Leo Dickinson) for page 19.
Hamish MacInnes for page 95.
Popperfoto for page 75.
Radio Times Hulton Picture Library for pages 24, 26 (2 & 3), 29, 34, 43, 44.
Royal Geographical Society/Mount Everest Foundation for pages 10, 22, 24, 25, 26 (bottom), 28, 31, 37, 38, 39 (bottom), 40, 41 (bottom), 42, 46, 74, 76.
Doug Scott for pages (vi-vii), 15 (left), 64 (both), 69, 70, 71, 88 (bottom), 90.
Times Newspapers Ltd for pages 45, 49.
Don Whillans for page 79.
Keiichi Yamada for page 58.

Extracts

Edward Arnold Ltd for the quotation on page 22 from G L Mallory's *Mount Everest: The Reconnaissance 1921* (1972).
John Napier and Jonathan Cape Ltd for the extracts on page 79 from John Napier's *Bigfoot* (1972).
Eric Shipton and Cassell & Co Ltd for the extract on page 31 from *Mountain Conquest* (1967).
Sir John Hunt and Hodder & Stoughton Ltd for the passages on pages 43-46 from Sir John's *The Ascent of Everest* (1953).
Sierra Club, San Francisco for the extract on page 55 from T Hornbein's *Everest: The West Ridge* (1968).
Dr Michael Ward for information contained in his article on pages 70-71 of *The Book of Modern Mountaineering* (Barker, 1968); Dr Ward and Eyre & Spottiswoode Ltd for the quotation from *The Mountaineer's Companion* (1966).

Maps and diagrams

Tim Smith
for the maps appearing at the beginning and end of the book:
    The Himalayas, with principal peaks
    Approach routes to Everest
    Kathmandu to Everest
    Everest
for the diagrams of mountaineering equipment on pages 2, 3, 5, 15.
for the geological diagrams on page 12.
for the Everest ascent-route diagrams on pages 54 and 67.

Index

113

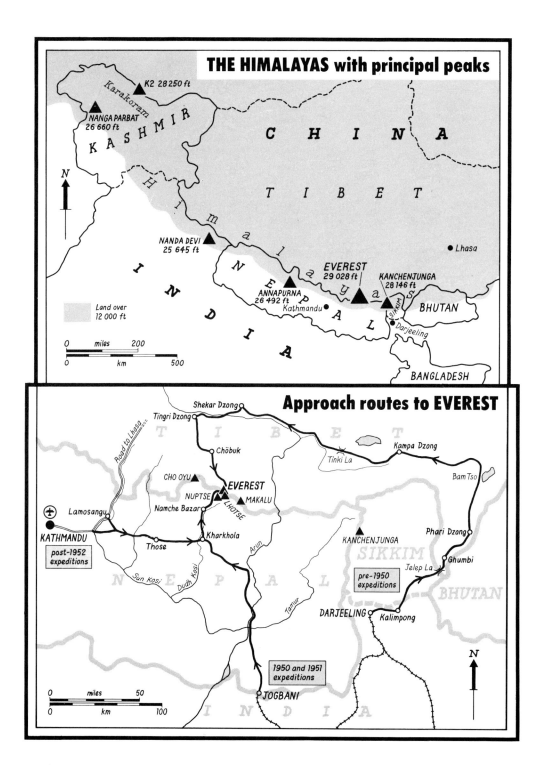

THE HIMALAYAS with principal peaks

Karakoram
K2 28 250 ft
NANGA PARBAT 26 660 ft
KASHMIR
CHINA
TIBET
H
i
m
a
l
NANDA DEVI 25 645 ft
a
y
NEPAL
EVEREST 29 028 ft
KANCHENJUNGA 28 146 ft
a
ANNAPURNA 26 492 ft
Kathmandu
• Lhasa
SIKKIM
BHUTAN
Darjeeling
INDIA
• Land over 12 000 ft
0   miles   200
0   km   500
BANGLADESH

Approach routes to EVEREST

Shekar Dzong
Tingri Dzong
Road to Lhasa
T   I   B   E   T
Chöbuk
Kampa Dzong
Tinki La
Bam Tso
CHO OYU
EVEREST
NUPTSE
MAKALU
LHOTSE
Namche Bazar
Lamosangu
Kharkhola
Arun
Phari Dzong
KANCHENJUNGA
Ghumbi
Jelep La
SIKKIM
KATHMANDU
post-1952 expeditions
Those
Sun Kosi
Dudh Kosi
N   E   P   A   L
pre-1950 expeditions
BHUTAN
Tamur
DARJEELING
Kalimpong
1950 and 1951 expeditions
0   miles   50
0   km   100
JOGBANI
I   N   D   I   A
N

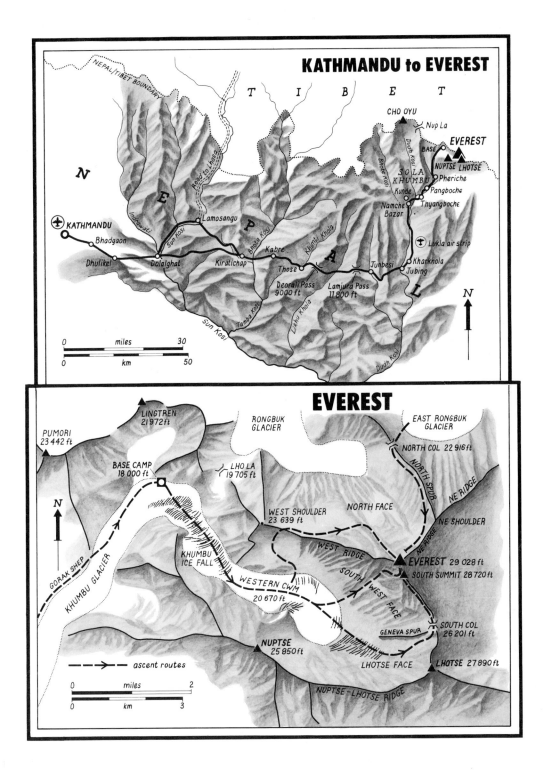

KATHMANDU to EVEREST

N

NEPAL/TIBET BOUNDARY

T I B E T

CHO OYU

Nup La

E V E R E S T

BASE

Dudh Kosi

NUPTSE LHOTSE

Road to Lhasa

Bhote Kosi

SOLA KHUMBU

Pheriche

Kunde

Pangboche

Namche Bazar

Thyangboche

Lamosangu

E P

Indrawati

KATHMANDU

Bhadgaon

Sun Kosi

Bhota Kosi

Kabre

Khimti Khola

Lukla air strip

Dhulikel

Dolalghat

Kiratichap

Those

A

Junbesi

Kharkhola

Jubing

L

Deorali Pass
9000 ft

Lamjura Pass
11 800 ft

Tamba Kosi

Likhu Khola

Sun Kosi

Dudh Kosi

N

| 0 | miles | 30 |
| 0 | km | 50 |

EVEREST

PUMORI
23 442 ft

LINGTREN
21 972 ft

RONGBUK
GLACIER

EAST RONGBUK
GLACIER

NORTH COL 22 916 ft

NORTH SPUR

NE RIDGE

BASE CAMP
18 000 ft

LHO LA
19 705 ft

WEST SHOULDER
23 639 ft

NORTH FACE

NE SHOULDER

N

KHUMBU
ICE FALL

WEST RIDGE

NE RIDGE

GORAK SHEP

KHUMBU GLACIER

WESTERN CWM
20 670 ft

SOUTH WEST FACE

EVEREST 29 028 ft

SOUTH SUMMIT 28 720 ft

GENEVA SPUR

SOUTH COL
26 201 ft

NUPTSE
25 850 ft

LHOTSE FACE

LHOTSE 27 890 ft

NUPTSE–LHOTSE RIDGE

- - -→ ascent routes

| 0 | miles | 2 |
| 0 | km | 3 |